EXCUSE ME
I'M JUST PASSING BY

by

David Belgum

Revised Edition 1999

Fairway Press, Lima, Ohio

CONTENTS

Other Post-Retirement Books by Belgum

Memoirs of Iowa's Only Socialist Mayor

The 5:08 and Other Stories

I Believe in God, Maker of All Things Visible and Invisible

Sometimes the Professor Preaches

Personality Portrait of a Parish

ACKNOWLEDGEMENTS

It helps to have other resources than one's own biased and defensive memory to go on in reconstructing one's life story. Several kinds of documents and a considerable collection of family photos helped to refresh my memory and provide accurate dates and experiential benchmarks. I also tried to use some of the methods from my textbook, *Religion and Personality in the Spiral of Life,* University Press of America, 1988.

Personal validation and reminiscences of brother Joe and sister Dorothy combined with some impressions and memories of cousins and other relatives added perspective. A visit to Starbuck and Glenwood, Minnesota, included conversations with Mrs. E.O. Barsness, the widow of my father's successor, and a group of his contemporaries whom she gathered for a nice luncheon.

I should also give thanks for my age as far as this task is concerned. I am writing from the perspective of retirement, and any judgments or opinions I now express will not influence my career nor jeopardize my marriage, will not increase or decrease the likelihood of my promotion or determine my salary. Many actors in supporting roles are long since dead and would not have their feelings hurt even if they disagreed with me. Having nothing to lose gives one a certain freedom from defensiveness and rationalization. Also, I have been blessed by a few therapeutic experiences which have helped me to become more objective about myself.

On the other hand, I was born a Norwegian Lutheran and suffer from all the consequences of that congenital birth defect. I have also been informed that I am full of Original Sin and the Old Adam, so do not expect perfection. Excuse me, that's just how it is.

Thanks to my wife, Kathie, for a critical reading and good suggestions. I am indebted to Linda Fisher for very close proofreading and stylistic improvements.

CHAPTER I

BEGINNING WITH MY HERITAGE

Excuse me, Dr. Carnahan, faithful osteopath of Glenwood, Minnesota, for having roused you out of your warm bed about midnight on the longest night of 1922. Yes, it was no little inconvenience that you had to hitch up your team to the sleigh and head south five miles to the Norwegian parsonage where Selma and Anton were anxiously awaiting your arrival, hoping it would coincide with my arrival. And there I was at 2:00 a.m. with a caul, sometimes called a victor's cap, covering my head. Mama took it as a good omen since it had also been the case with some great people: Julius Caesar, Napoleon Bonaparte and David Copperfield, for example.

Healthcare in Glenwood was neatly divided between two disciplines. Dr. Carnahan took care of childbirth, surgery, cutting and like that; whereas, Dr. Witts, the chiropractor, provided health maintenance, adjustment and generic treatments. Even mentioning the name of Dr. Witts conjures up memories of classic sessions of what we later came to call psychosomatic medicine. One such incident stands out.

Mama and I were sitting in the waiting room in such a way that I could see clearly, through a crack in the doorway, how Dr. Witts was dealing with Mrs. Swenson. He was diagnosing her case by means of a huge, radio-like instrument. It had large black knobs, which he adjusted with his left hand while the three center fingers of his right hand slid back and forth over a piece of slate, giving off a screechy noise. Meanwhile, Mrs. Swenson sat upright in a high-backed wooden chair holding a metal ring in each hand. Strapped to her forehead was a metal plate about three inches in diameter. Indicators at several locations flickered like the needle on a dashboard indicating that you are low on gas. Mrs. Swenson was low on gas.

Dr. Witts combined information gained from casual chatter together with his scientific instrumentation to arrive at a diagnosis. She had shared, with drawn countenance, how it had not been easy cooking for a threshing crew of eighteen, slopping the hogs while the men were all out in the fields and caring for the three kids who were eighteen, thirty-six and fifty-four months old respectively. The diagnosis came together in Dr. Witts' keen mind with confident precision. "You don't suppose you've been over-doing?" She slapped her thigh and said with relief, "I bet that's it!" This was an insight that her stoical Norse husband, Lars, would never have glimpsed even though they had been married almost five years. But there was more to the treatment before she would hand over the two dollars, which she felt was well worth it.

Next, she, like everyone else, stretched out on a waist-high table covered with oilcloth. She had her back massaged and her head twisted sharply from side to side. Her spine was rotated and gotten back into "adjustment," and that was that. Lars had not done that since their honeymoon.

The final stage of therapy was to sit in a small compartment about the size of a phone booth. There Mrs. Swenson would hold metal rings as before and have the metal disc strapped to her forehead. In ten to fifteen minutes this gave a nice closure to the session, because it was like completing a cycle. It was also the first time she had had permission to sit down since the harvest began.

When Mrs. Swenson returned to the waiting room, an unstructured group therapy session was getting into high gear. An absent sister's case was being reviewed after it was fully explained why she had not come for her treatment this Saturday.

"Ja, you know how it has been with her; she always vas like dat," an older woman remarked. This was followed by a shrewd diagnostic statement: "It is not surprising; you know she vas illegally born."

Mrs. Swenson would have liked to have stayed for more details, but Lars would be waiting for her parked in front of the Savings Bank.

At the other end of Lake Minnewaska, about ten miles west, was the small village of Starbuck. There, providing excellent surgery in a minuscule hospital, was a legitimate M.D., whose name I shall not mention because he had a fairly large problem with alcohol. I had my encounter with him at age three when I developed a nasty mastoid condition. Long before penicillin, sulfa and other wonder drugs were created or discovered, the cure for this infection was to carve out the affected bone area and sanitize it best you could. Mama highly disapproved of alcoholism; but at least he was a Norwegian Lutheran and the best surgeon anywhere on the prairie horizon. He greeted her at the hospital with bleary eyes and hangover breath. He also sensed immediately Mama's concern about handing over her little boy to this kind of person. He said calmly and reassuringly, "Don't worry Mrs. Belgum; everything will be all right." He disappeared into his dressing room and returned in a little while bright eyed and bushy tailed. Evidently he had taken one of the amphetamines; and Mama was grateful. I was too, because sixty-seven years later, the scar behind my right ear is hardly noticeable. He went deep enough, but not too deep, thanks to his wonderful antidote. It is important to treat the surgeon as well as the patient.

Why do I get sidetracked onto medicine and health care so early in my life's history? I guess it was central in many ways. First, Papa traded in the old Model T Ford, with side curtains, for the draft-proof 1926 Chevrolet with roll-up windows. I often heard this was so David would not get a draft on his ear and get sick again. Also, I did not learn how to swim properly in Lake Minnewaska, because, if I got water in my ear, I would wind up with an earache fairly soon. Mama used to say, "Take care of your health; it's the most precious possession you have." As far back as I can remember I had an aversion to violent, physical contact sports such as football and boxing, neither of which is conducive to health of nose, knees and rib cage. You be the judge of whether it was caution or cowardice.

My physical proportions and general metabolism were quite normal from birth onward. What I inherited from my ancestors is of formative significance in my life. That is why it is important to take time out in this story to clue you in on what they were like. I have already implied that I came from Norwegian stock and grew up in a Norwegian Lutheran rural ghetto.

The grandparent about whom I know most, and whom I always considered as a great character role model, is Hans Johnshoy, my mother's father. For a pioneer farmer, education had been a major part of his life. Back in Norway he had attended a rotating school until age fourteen. Its rotation consisted of being conducted for one week in each of the neighboring farm houses. He was an assistant teacher for three years, and the neighbors urged him to attend the normal school to become a certified teacher. Hans was too conservative to go into debt for such a venture and, instead, chose to emigrate to America as other young Norwegians were doing in large numbers.

Hans Johnshoy
1847–1937

The poignant farewells were said with mother and sisters, and the father walked with the twenty-year-old Hans to the edge of a long frozen lake where a sleigh took him to the train station and the thirty-five mile ride to the harbor, then called Christiania. The conversation on that fifteen-mile walk was their last as the father died two years later.

What stamina it must have taken to cross the Atlantic. Each passenger had to bring his/her own food, no doubt a sack for hardtack and brown bread and another for cured summer sausage. Then, you could only hope that drinking water would last for the seven weeks before the sailing ship finally docked in Quebec. As the presiding minister, the captain buried eight children at sea, as the little bodies were sewn into sailcloth with sand enough to sink them into the deep, cold grave, and a brief liturgy was read.

While other passengers roiled in seasickness, Hans found a sailor who helped him learn English an hour a day. He had brought a new Norse-English dictionary and mastered twenty new words a day, as he said in his memoirs, "both spelling and meaning." He acculturated so quickly that he even taught several years in one-room country schoolhouses in Wisconsin and Minnesota.

After working in several jobs in Wisconsin, he decided to visit some acquaintances in Pope County, Minnesota. Again, stamina was called for. He walked thirty miles to La Crosse, Wisconsin, to catch a steamer up to Saint Paul and thence by train to Saint Cloud. But from there he had to walk seventy-five miles across the prairie to reach his destination further west. He had hoped to reach it in two days, but a storm interrupted his walk.

When his widowed mother and a sister came to join him in America, they all decided to settle in Minnesota. Again the journey, this time with ox cart, crossing the swollen Mississippi, and the hazard of the semi-trained oxen almost capsizing their cart while it was being loaded on the ferry. The Minnesota River they crossed on a log raft, and the sodden swamps they traversed as best they could. With typically reverent and positive attitude, he wrote, "However, we arrived safely without losing anything, and so had every reason to be thankful to God." They had made the journey in four weeks. It would not even take that long to cover the four hundred miles today on the super highway, comforted by a heater in the winter or an air conditioner in the summer.

Sober-sided Norwegians did not waste a lot of romance on marriage. Hans and Mari were no exception as per this quote from his memoirs:

> The pastor gave us an urgent admonition from God's Word, to
> hold fast to that in life's storms, then our marriage would be like
> a grapevine that clings to the strong trunk of a tree ... The young
> wife took hold with thrift and moderation ... (lacking lace
> curtains) she used newspapers and succeeded so well that
> strangers driving by thought they were the real thing.

(More about Grandma later.)

Thrift and moderation were more important on the prairie than beauty and other frivolities. Their "claim shanty" was not large-- 12 x 14 x 8.

Out of a dozen children, half died before the age of two. That's enough to sober you up right there. The parents worked through their grief tangibly: Put the child in a simple pine box, dig a hole and have the minister say the liturgy including casting earth on the casket three times with the somber words:

> *Af Jord er du kommen.*
> *Til Jord skal du blive.*
> *Af Jorden skal du igjen opstaae.*

From the earth you are come.
To the earth shall you return.
From the earth shall you rise up again.

With each sentence the pastor cast another spade full of dirt upon the little homemade casket. They worked with the grief themselves because they had no undertaker to pass it off to. They faced it openly and with the support of their neighbors--no prettifying, no denial--faced it head on and went on to the next task of life.

Financially and vocationally this farm family was a success. After forty years, they handed the farm over to their son, Herman, and moved into the nearby village of Starbuck where they built their retirement house on twenty acres on the northwest corner of the growing town. Selling off lots was part of their pension plan.

Hans was asked to serve as "klokker" in the church. It involved two tasks: leading the singing before reed organs were popular and praying the *Indgangsbön* (prayer of preparation before entering into the Service) in Norwegian:

> Lord! we have come into your holy house to hear what you …
> will tell us. Lord! open our hearts, by your Holy Spirit, so that
> we may learn from your Word to repent of our sins, to believe in
> Jesus in life and in death, and to grow day by day in grace and
> holiness.

Only then did the Pastor come before the altar to begin the *Höimessegudstjeneste* (literally High Mass of God's Service). After Hans had done this for twenty-five years, the congregation gave him an elegant gold, Elgin pocket watch with a hinged cover for the face and a double cover on the back, the second one covering the fifteen jewel works. The inscription on this watch, which I cherish to this day, is shown below.

To
H. Johnshoy
from
Immanuel Congregation
1899

My father's side of the family was also 100 percent Norwegian. I visited the Belgum farm in Norway where my grandfather was born. It is on such a steep hillside that there is no way a car nor a carriage could drive up to the house. The hay was hung up to dry because the mist from the surrounding waterfalls was so dense. The farms are so small that it is understandable there would not be enough land for all the sons who might wish to farm. Valdres Valley is about three hours train ride northwest of Oslo. Getting off at the Fagernes station on a beautiful lakeshore was a summer's delight. A phone call located an Olaf Belgum, who invited me to come to his *pensionat* for coffee. On a long shelf in the dining room was an impressive row of ski-jumping trophies, especially the one he got for winning the competition at the famous *Holmenkollbakken* on the outskirts of Oslo. On either side of the ski-jump site are two extensive sets of bleachers. The jumpers glide onto the frozen lake after landing. Norwegians are great outdoors people.

Olaf and his wife drove me to the parish church where my grandfather was baptized at a font beautifully carved in the form of an angel holding a seashell. The church was built in 1250 A.D. In the cemetery was a tombstone marking the resting place of a Lieutenant Belgum, "Killed by a Swede - 1817." Ouch! The old church was built of stone with walls about thirty inches thick. A course of such stones was laid and the center filled in with dirt. A gradual ramp incline made it possible to drag the next layer up and put them in place. When the roof was completed, they simply excavated all the dirt and it was finished. A clever invention before hydraulic lifts. The whole trip gave me a feeling for my roots, roots that went deep into mountains and valleys, forests and meadows--and history. After all, this valley was the last holdout against King Olav's attempt to Christianize Norway. When a mob had him cornered, he sent some of his soldiers to set their homes on fire across the lake. When the locals scurried to save their homes, he escaped. That was in 1023 A.D. He also threatened, "Get baptized or have your heads cut off."

Norse ways and myths continued even in my father's parish. Once he came to a farmyard and was shocked to see the farm wife churning butter, but with one leg of the churn resting on the family Bible. "Could you not brace up the churn by resting that leg on a board?" he wanted to know. "That is not it, Pastor," she explained. "If the churn sits on the Word, the Nisse and Trolls in the woods cannot keep it from turning into butter." And it was true. If you rested the churn on the Bible and cranked the handle very fast, it always turned into butter. Troublemakers south of Glenwood were also referred to as *Streels,* spirits who lived in the forest and associated with other things that went bump in the night, stirring up trouble and mischief.

Papa had felt greatly honored to be invited to give the major address at the *Valdristevnet* in Minneapolis in 1911, just a year after he was ordained. Some at this convention of Valdres descendants of immigrants, as well as those born in the valley itself, said that Pastor Belgum had the purest Valdres dialect of anyone around.

Grandpa Henrick Belgum served some military time in Norway and won a medal as a marksman. He also jumped into the harbor and rescued a man from drowning. But when I asked Papa why his father, a pioneer farmer in Pope County, Minnesota, died so young, in his early fifties, I got a rather vague and brief answer: "Stomach trouble." I never found out if it was stomach ulcer, stomach cancer, or a knife in the stomach. At any rate he was gone before I was born.

Henrick and his wife Britt followed the architectural path of most pioneers on the prairie: First a sod hut dug into a sidehill with logs for a roof covered by a thick layer of sod, sometimes oiled paper for windows; next came the log house above ground with maybe two rooms and a loft for the children to sleep in; and then wood siding to cover the logs and dress up the place as well as add some insulation.

Neither did I get to know my paternal grandmother. It was not until I was well into my twenties that I understood the somewhat strange relationship of Aunt Alma to the rest of the family. She was born a couple years after Grandpa died and Britt had never remarried. It was another thirty years, when I preached at a big family reunion at Nora Church, north of Starbuck, that I learned that Britt had been buried, not beside her husband, but at his feet to signify the shame of the error of her ways. Shame, guilt and bearing grudges were all part of the staple diet of the grim Norwegians. Garrison Keillor once said of the Norwegian Lutheran farmers in Lake Wobegon that sins were not so much to be forgiven as to be treasured so that they could be dredged up and viewed from time to time. "I tink it vas seventeen years ago dis spring dat she did dat. Ja, it vas too bad how it vent vit her."

The contemporary form of the opening confessional prayer goes like this: "... we poor sinners confess unto Thee, that we are by nature sinful and unclean, and that we have sinned against Thee by thought, word and deed."

The old Norwegian liturgy was even more ominous.

> *... er ganske og aldeles strafskyldig og fordommelig.* (... we are wholly and absolutely deserving of punishment and condemnable.)

We Norwegians took for granted that this would be our condition every Sunday morning even though the last Sunday's service had ended with the Benediction, "The Lord bless thee ... and give thee peace." This optimistic prophecy was never expected to be fulfilled. Each Sunday morning we were minus ten again on a moral scale of minus ten for big trouble in "thought, word and deed," on the one hand, and plus ten for being mightily blessed. No one ever even made it up to a plus two like many Methodists and others of more cheerful denominations did.

To understand me and the rest of my ilk, you must grasp this dark mood, this self-effacing pessimism as a life-style. It was not only in religion. When a hostess had created a county fair first-prize cake for dessert, and all the guests knew it for sure, she was somehow obligated to say, "You'll have to excuse the cake; it doesn't usually fall together like that." It was the negative etiquette of lying in a good cause. The cause was to avoid the sin of pride at all costs. At a sumptuous feast, "Pick together and make what you can of it."

Scandinavians rank very high in suicides, the ultimate in low self-esteem and anger turned inward against the self. The Italians in a sunnier clime are so spontaneous and outgoing that they have many fewer suicides and are sensible enough to direct their anger outward, hence, more murders. Maybe that is why there is no Norwegian Mafia; the "hit man" would end up shooting himself instead of the contracted and intended victim.

Maybe a better way of illustrating the character traits of my grandparents' generation than trying to describe them is to show you the visages of an assortment of their contemporaries. The photo in the upper left-hand corner of the following page depicts my maternal grandmother, Mari. The one in the lower right-hand corner, I am told, was the mother of a *Streel*. It is my guess that none of them sang the cute little Sunday School song, "Brighten the corner where you are."

You might ask how such religion and temperament could possibly have supported those pioneers in their adverse conditions. It may not have been a sentimental or exhibitionist faith; but it was rock solid. Perhaps it was even combined with some of that Norse fatalism, so often typified by, "It was meant to be."

Norwegian Lutheran Pioneer Countenances

1. "I think I have enough to top it with."
"Yes, that'll be just right."

2. "Does it look pretty good? Maybe you'll go and get the ladder, Ola." "It looks as if I had set it up myself."

3. "I'm coming right away." "Oh, there's no hurry."

4. "You don't need to bring the ladder, Ola. I think I made it down all right."

Norse pioneers were serious, but they could also laugh at themselves in these cartoons.

From *Han Ola og han Per* by Peter Rosendahl
and edited by Joan Buckley and Einar Haugen. Courtesy of
Universitetsforlaget, Oslo, Norway

Consider a few excerpts from Hans Johnshoy's memoirs where he comments on the loss of their first four children. On a modest stone marker in the country church yard is inscribed, "Children born of parents Hans and Mari Johnshoy--Blessed are the dead who die in the Lord" (in Norwegian, naturally).

> Our marriage was blessed by a son, who got the name Johan. It pleased the Lord to call him home when he was a month old. We felt a great loss and had to learn to say: "The Lord gave, the Lord took, blessed be the name of the Lord." A year later we got a daughter, Clara Mina.... A couple years later we got another daughter, Caroline Elisabet. She was sickly and died three months old. This was a great blow to us. Yet when we had thought it over, we had to say: "God does all things well." Next time we got a boy, Joseph Engvald, very hale and hearty.... But that year diphtheria raged over a large part of the state, and tore away many children. Our two caught the disease and died within two days of each other, so they were buried on the same day. Thus all our children were torn away from us and we were left with sorely wounded hearts. Then it was good to remember that "I know my Redeemer lives.

Marriages almost always lasted "till death do us part." The wife worked as hard as the husband to make a go of it. There was almost no discussion about burnout or identity crisis. If the parents died, the children went to live with the Godparents, who had already promised at the infant's baptism to rear the child in a godly way if the need arose--no need for a "home study" by a social worker to see if the sod hut met state standards. Rights were few and far between, but responsibilities were everywhere. Not that there were no problems, including mental problems and handicaps, but mostly you just took it on the chin, heaved an accepting sigh and went on with plowing, harvesting, breastfeeding the last baby and knitting another sweater before winter set in. You also took the grasshoppers, the drought and hail and blizzards for granted as part of nature. Why fuss? It was all under God's sovereignty anyway as you confess in the First Article of the Nicene Creed: "I believe in one God, the Father Almighty, Maker of heaven and earth, and of all things visible and invisible."

From my ancestors I have inherited this stoical religious perspective on life. It was also sturdy stock, i.e., among those who passed the test for survival of the fittest on the bleak prairie. Mama and her parents all lived into their nineties and Papa lived to eighty-eight. Outside of some minor items, I have been remarkably healthy until now, my seventieth year.

I have found Grundtvig's saying stimulating: "I am first a Dane and second a Christian." By this he meant that he was first born into a particular time and place, historically and geographically, with its unique weather, soils, folk myths, customs and temperament. Secondly, he and I were baptized in infancy into the Kingdom of God with all that entails. So now let's get back to when and where I was born.

CHAPTER II

PARSONAGE LIFE

I was born December 22, 1922, the same year that *Reader's Digest* was born. Remember the "Roaring Twenties" when loose women bobbed their hair and tried out their cigarette holders? I was protected from booze while in the parsonage because Prohibition covered the years 1919 through 1933 when the Irish got back their national pastime. Meanwhile there were speak-easies where those on the in could speak the password. Papa was not amused when a certain establishment was opened near the flour mill on the shore of a dammed-up pond across from his Chippewa Falls Lutheran Church and was given the shady name of "Tavern by a Dam Site."

Two approaches emerged from this parsonage as far as alcoholism was concerned. After a fairly wild box-lunch social at the nearby country schoolhouse, a young Norwegian farmer got drunk. My mother bundled him into the back of our sleigh and hauled him home to the parsonage and put him to bed. The next morning a place was set for him at the dining table (usually reserved for festive occasions) with a white linen tablecloth and the best dishes and silver. While the young man shamefacedly ate his delicious breakfast, my mother sat opposite him and simply looked him right in his hangover face without saying a word during the entire meal. He was reported to have said he would rather have gone to jail. My father took a more direct approach to another person who had trouble with alcohol. "Lars! If you don't stop drinking, I won't bury you." I never heard if it cured him.

The above illustrations are cited as an example of the central role of the Norwegian Lutheran parsonage in those days.

The schoolteacher often boarded at the Pastor's house because it was a seat of learning and culture. Papa urged that a "Yankee" be hired as a teacher so the kids would learn English without an accent. Mother was more or less in charge of social work and pastoral care, as most ministers' wives were in those days. I was older before I understood why we always seemed to have a "hired girl" even though we couldn't afford one. They'd stay a few months before "going to Minneapolis for awhile" (translate Lutheran Girls' Home where the baby was usually put up for adoption). Then Mama would line up some eligible bachelor from the parish, and that took care of that.

Choir practice took place in our living room, Mama serving as organist and pianist. Some visits were social and genial; others were solemn and confidential as a repentant or disciplined parishioner slid out the front door where he/she had come in.

Missions Fest, an annual event for stimulating interest in support of foreign missions, was a highlight of the year. The missionary, and maybe his wife, would stay a few days and preach on Sunday as well as show his lantern slides one evening. These were brittle, glass-encased black and white objects, about four inches square, through which an intense light was projected. On the screen were projected the headhunters and other wild ones from Natambanana, Natal; Papua New Guinea; Madagascar; Alaska, etc. The pornography of bare-breasted native women was not deemed dangerous to a young boy such as myself since the subjects were totally black and it was assumed I would make no connection with totally white, blond Norwegian females such as were all around me in the parish. On top of that, the purpose was evangelism and the noble goal was getting the women to wear blouses and dresses and the men to wear pants and hats. It was, after all, a missionary program to "take up the white man's burden." Yes, indeed, the parsonage was an interesting place.

A large, square, corner room on the first floor was Papa's Study. There was a large roll-top desk, some bookcases and a huge leather rocking chair with wide wooden runners and arm rests. In the corner, behind that chair, was my hideaway where I would look at exotic pictures. I still own Papa's Volume V of Matthew Henry's commentary on the Bible published in 1811. It was still a respected resource when Papa was a student at the Norwegian Lutheran Seminary in Saint Paul in the first decade of this century. Gory illustrations and engravings fascinated me most. For example, the picture, on the following page, of the beheading of John was very dramatic with the woman holding out the platter to receive the trophy (yuch!). This was from Matthew 14:10.

Another engraving that transfixed me was one depicting how Satan is escaping from his cage in the dungeon for a final blast against the faithful in the "end time." It seemed to be a composite from the Book of Revelation with the Devil, the Dragon, the Anti-Christ, and every slimy evil thing rolled into one. It was a most gruesome creature, and I am sure I wondered some nights, before falling asleep, if this would be the night he would break out and raise hell all over the county. Knowing that God could see right through the ceiling, even in the dark, did not help any. And then there was the constant assurance that you were in big trouble in "thought, word, and deed." If there was anyone this monster should have for breakfast, it was maybe my humble Norwegian self.

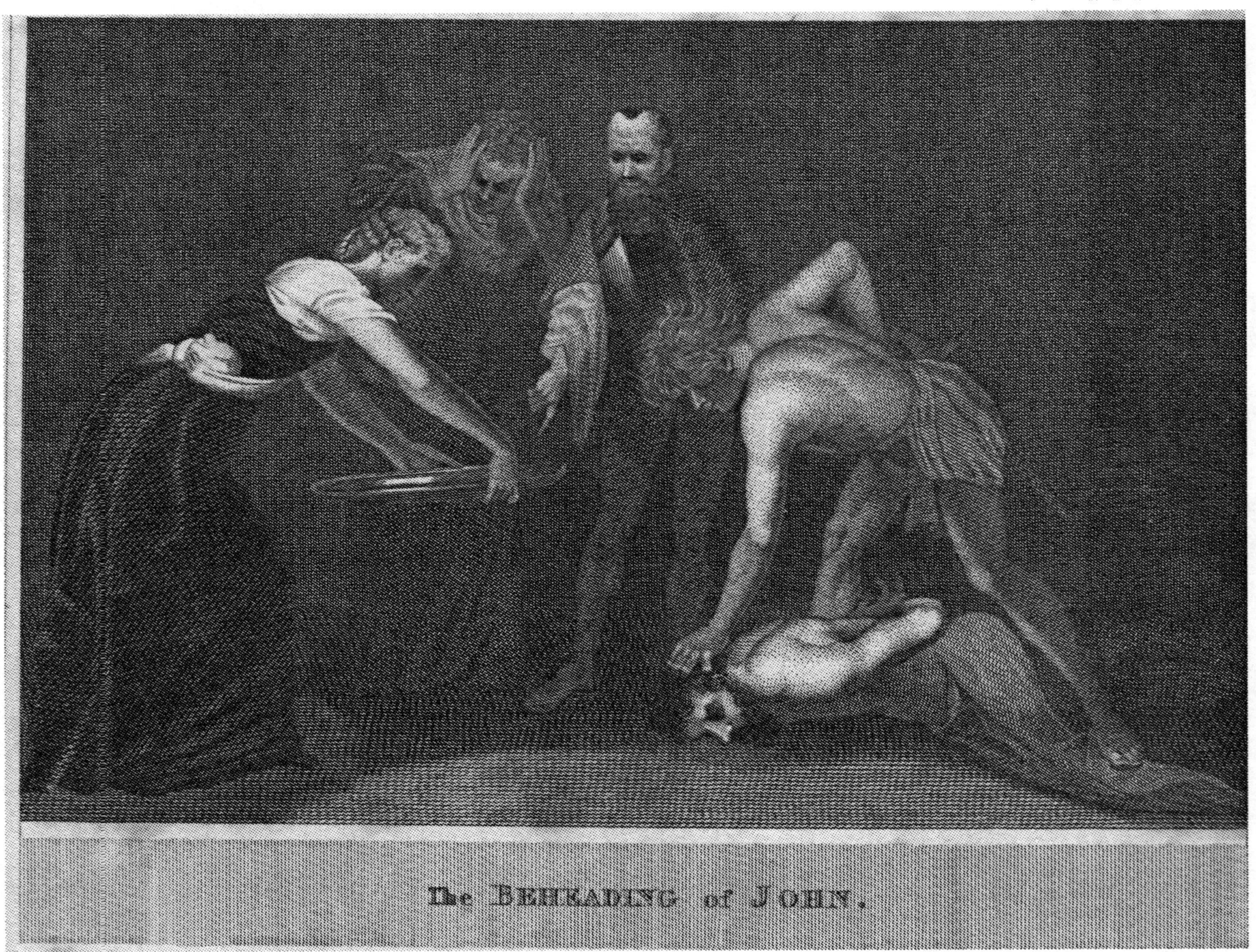

The BEHEADING of JOHN.

The Twenties constituted an interesting decade in which to begin my life. George Gershwin wrote "Rhapsody in Blue." The Scopes Trial about teaching evolution in public schools resulted in a $100 fine for the teacher. Charles Lindbergh flew solo to Paris. There were scandals then as now--in those days the Teapot Dome Scandal. Finally the decade ended with the Stock Market crash on Wall Street. So much for the historical setting and the times.

Getting back to the parsonage and the twenty acres of land that went with it calls for a historical footnote. *Prestegard,* pastor's yard or pastor's farm, was a Scandinavian institution. Back in Norway the pastor was employed by the state since it was a state church. Above a good salary, he had other perquisites, one of which was to have the use of a farm and tenants to go with it. He was entitled to the income and also was thereby considered part of the landed gentry. Being a university graduate like the doctors and lawyers, he also had considerable social status. Add to this his "holy calling" and he was definitely a cut above the majority of the citizens, one might even say alienated from the masses.

When the early immigrants finally obtained a pastor of their own for the newly formed two-congregation parish (White Bear Lake and Chippewa Falls churches), it was time to create as much of a *prestegard* as they could. That meant a sizable house and a barn for two cows and two horses plus twenty acres for hay and a pasture for the same. Only minus the tenant farmer.

Papa and Mama moved into this impressive house (at least I thought it was) about a dozen years after it was built. Maybe the reason the pastor's salary started at $900 a year was the confident hope that this vast farm of twenty acres would bring in quite a living. And it did in a way. We had a large garden, had our own eggs, milk and home-churned butter. Then the cows took turns having a calf, which meant having fresh meat on a continuous basis. Papa took on a sideline of raising turkeys and even won first prize for an enormous tom at the State Fair, which he sold for $25.00, big money back then. My brother, Joe, was five years older than I. We both showed vegetables at the county fair. One year he had a lamb and I exhibited a handsome white Wyandotte rooster and two hens (first prize if you please). Some farmer parishioners were jealous and did not believe I had actually raised them, which I had done. One was heard to say, "That just shows some kids got smart folks." The parsonage was a healthy place in which to grow from birth well into the third grade, when we departed from the parsonage.

First permanent parsonage built in 1902. Rev. Bale and Ferdinand

Although the photo of the parsonage and the barn shows an absolutely flat plain in the background, two features are not present in the picture. One is the impressive double row of evergreens Papa planted along the entire north side of the yard and also across the west side to protect the barn and house from winter blasts. To the left of the photo were two creek hills leading down to a pleasant stream with an occasional willow to set off the view. It was great to slide down one side, across the frozen stream, and halfway up the other hill as a winter sport. In the summer I herded minnows with a stick like a cowboy trying to get them into a corral.

Browsing through our family album, I see pictures of me, when I was almost twice as tall as a turkey gobbler, feeding the flock with great dignity and self-importance. Another shows me explaining Joe's lamb to a city-slicker cousin from Seattle. The poor guy hardly knew anything at all.

Papa gave me the important job of being his "Lantern Man" at milking time. Especially in the winter this was necessary because it got dark so early. I remember one such trip to the barn as though it were this evening. When I was five, I would have told it like this:

Now as Papa opens the barn door, top and bottom together in the winter, I smell the sweet alfalfa hay from last summer. And it's warm in the barn, too. The steam from the cows' breathing hits the nail heads in the boards and makes a white frost stick out all over. Whenever there is a hole it fills up with frost. Papa says that's why it's so warm in here--the heat from the two horses and the two cows. You can see it clear as anything where my lantern shines on it.

Papa hangs the lantern up high so we can see everything from the cow's manger to the poop pile she made near the door. Papa shovels it out so the stink won't get into the milk. You can't train a cow more'n so much. This brown and white one we can't even train to keep her tail still when Papa milks her. So that's my next job, to hold the cow's tail still so's it won't switch Papa in the face when he's sitting alongside her on the milk stool. Oh, it's not as bad as in the summer with all the flies bitin' her here and there, now just does it out of habit, I guess. Hard to break a person of a habit. I gotta be careful not to hold her tail too tight either or she kicks something fierce and the whole pail will go flyin' like it did last summer once. Papa still lets me do this job even though I made a mistake that time. I don't like it much when she gets poop on the end of her tail, but I guess it's better to get it on my hands than in Papa's face especially tonight when Mama will be having choir practice in the living room by the time we get back from the milking. I'll just rub it off in the snow on the way back to the house and nobody will be the wiser--unless they can smell it, of course.

Well, everything's going pretty good in the barn and the pail is over half full. Papa looks pleased. He takes the lantern off the hook and hands it to me just like he knows what I'll do with it. He trusts me a lot with this lantern. He looks around to see everything is OK and we head for the door. The lantern handle is a little slippery but I close my fingers around it so the brown stuff won't show. Papa says, "Well, Lantern Man, let's go."

On the way to the house I bend over enough to pick up some snow for my hand cleaning job, but the lantern drags on the snow bank and it looks like it's going to go out. Papa looks around, but by that time I catch my balance and walk along like everything is just fine. Oh well, I can always clean up in the house.

When Papa puts the milk in the cellar, Mama calls out to me to come into the living room and meet the new organist who is sitting at the piano looking like a new fresh ironed pillow case. The choir is standing over by the davenport.

"Oh, so you're little David, the pastor's boy," she says in a loud voice that sounds like she's gargling. She holds out her hand in a quick way that makes me jump; and before I know it I shake that hand. I slip out of her grasp leaving a shiny brown mark between her thumb and other fingers.

It's not easy being a lantern man, like tonight fer instance.

Ah yes, I could not have asked for a better place to be born nor a more accepting and loving family to be born into. Fresh air and plenty of food, freedom to come and go in safety, a chance to dig in the earth and get acquainted with nature. Papa was especially interested in nature from trees and cattle to the Roman and Greek names for the constellations he pointed out to us on clear nights. This poem he wrote in his retirement shows his keen interest and observation of details in nature, in this case the sparrow. It grows out of Matthew 6:26.

> They gather not into granary with sorrow,
> Nor are anxious for the morrow.
> Jesus solemnly said of birds, including the sparrow.
>
> Do not be anxious for the morrow,
> Nor be worried in this world with sorrow,
> For ye are worth more than a sparrow.
>
> Above the mouth is the narrow nose;
> The food to reject or to choose.
>
> Above--the two bright, brown eyes;
> The entrance to guard like two spies.
>
> The tongue at the bottom lies;
> The food (before eating) tests, tastes, and tries.
>
> Of molars and eyeteeth, have not any;
> But stones in the gizzard, they have many.
>
> Not like us, worry and work so hard,
> But against evil enemies always on the guard.
>
> The feathers flush to the body match,
> Grow and change from the day they hatch.
>
> Against the wind they turn and wait,
> So down fold the feathers flat and straight.
>
> The feathers on the back overlap each other
> Like the shingles on the roof shed water.
>
> The soft skin is warm in winter weather,
> The snowstorm they can meet and weather.

The wings forward propel on either side,
The tail does the flight direct and guide.

During summer vacation he would take us all to a cabin in Itasca State Park where we could step across the headwaters of the Mississippi on stones or a little wooden bridge, where we could feed deer a piece of toast through a fence and much more. It was a solid wholesome kind of entertainment, not frivolous or wasteful. I can still visualize Papa relaxing in front of the cabin, sitting fairly erect with a white shirt, black vest and tie and dress-up straw hat. Most of our activities were either useful, like weeding the garden, or educational, like learning the difference between the nominative and dative case ("John hit the ball. <u>He</u> hit the ball to <u>him</u>.") Such grammar drills were started earlier than first grade, sometimes while milking. From the picture (p. 31) you will notice that he had white hair, being almost forty by the time I was born.

Mama was the cheerful and optimistic side of the pair. I always think of her countenance as friendly and warm, like in the photo taken in later years.

Even when the family had to move time and again in unsettling conditions, she would explain to my young sister, Dorothy, "Won't it be exciting to move to ________. Think of how many new friends you'll make and new things you'll see." Her morals and standards were very clear, but they were matched by grace, forgiveness, and love (often missing among highly moral Norwegians).

My two brothers were five and ten years older than I. Joe and I together went to the country school, District 78, but Harold was already boarding with a family in Glenwood to attend high school, and after that went to Luther College. So I was not as close to him in my childhood. I doubt if there was much sibling rivalry because we competed in such different spheres. Harold was the scholar with straight A's. Joe was the athlete in basketball, football, and boxing. And I excelled in stuttering, which I will explain shortly.

Sister Dorothy was born six months before we left the parsonage. Mama steadied herself on my shoulder in the last months of pregnancy and called me her "leaning post." Both parents had nice ways of making me feel wanted, needed, and important. Mama's health was frail in some ways, which explains why the children were spaced well apart (1911, 1917, 1922 and 1930). She told me Papa was very considerate of her, and they practiced planned parenthood, "<u>coitus interruptus</u>," as she explained it. It was as bold as she ever got on "that topic," but Papa would have never discussed such an intimate subject any more than he would have discussed the state of his soul life. Some things you just don't talk about either because they are too holy or too "baas" or "fishda"--anything pertaining to urine, feces or sex, etc.

Our family was always supportive of each other. Our parents encouraged us in whatever endeavors we had in mind.

Perhaps Papa, especially, was sensitive to the negative consequences of forcing a person into a vocation--rather let it be a totally free choice. They valued education and we all went at least one degree beyond our BAs. Harold's teaching position at Mission House College secured tuition for his kid brother Joe. They both helped me; and, if I remember correctly, we helped sister Dorothy when we could. Finally, since Papa never owned a house (the parsonage system putting a pastor in the category of a permanent tenant), we all pitched in to pay for their apartment rent, funeral expenses, etc. Thus we came full circle. Not one of us ever kept track of these transactions because money was never highly valued in our family. I have always been grateful for this heritage because I have seen so many families torn apart by covetousness and jealousy. Especially sad are the fights that take place at the funeral of the patriarch or rich relative as the children (yes, acting like little kids) squabble over the "goodies" in the inheritance.

Since Dorothy and I were about eight years apart in age, we were not close siblings in the early years. Later, like when I was in the Seminary and she was attending high school in Minneapolis, we did things together. She reminded me of the time I invited her to a seminary Christmas party and occasions when we attended plays and concerts. We continued to become closer as the years went on.

Over holidays, we got involved in projects like insulating a back porch in a North Dakota parsonage so Mama's laundry would not freeze stiff in the washing machine. This is as good a place as any to acknowledge my indebtedness to all my siblings as well as to my parents for the gifts of belonging and caring.

The family photo portrays security and success, peace and stability both in the parsonage and in the parish. I was about four years old at the time. To me the parsonage was somewhere between a palace and a castle, prestigious and impregnable. What a life! Somewhere about this time the mood changed, but that's another story.

Rev. and Mrs. Belgum, Harold, Joseph, and David

CHAPTER III

TROUBLE FOR THE PASTOR
and a
P-P-P-PR-PRO-PROBLEM FOR M-M-ME

Things had been going along pretty smoothly for the six-foot handsome, proper and articulate pastor for a dozen years. Then, as sometimes happens, the honeymoon with the parish is long gone and rumblings of dissatisfaction can be heard from the back pews, and even some in the front pew hold their pocket watch to their ear to see if it is time that has stood still or the sermon. Could there have been underground resentments about the building project at Chippewa Falls (1927) when the church was jacked up and a basement inserted underneath? It has been folk wisdom that the pastor should leave shortly after a major building project has been completed. Shortly after the joyous notes of the doxology fade away at the dedication, the echo can be heard: "But it cost too much - much - much"; "What we had before was good enough for my folks and it was good enough for me - me - me"; "It could have been spent on missions, -ons, -ons, -ons." Yes, echoing across the pond and bouncing back from Tavern by a Dam Site.

A common understanding, whether true or not I cannot attest, was that certain members felt they knew when a "minister had stayed long enough" and then proceeded to usher him out the door. A member told my father's successor that he would last ten years. Why? "Because that's how long I thought I'd like you." Could it again be a touch of that Nordic fatalism? Now my Papa was not one to seek out counsel from the District President on how to handle rumblings or trouble or troublemakers. According to Lutheran polity, you were called to a parish for life and only moved if another call came along, i.e., a call came spontaneously in the mail. It would be forward to "seek" a call, not to trust the Holy Spirit, to negotiate or play church politics. No! One simply stayed and did one's duty day by day, sermon by sermon, funeral by funeral until another call would lead you elsewhere. Antagonism is one parish illness that does not heal itself. Things got grimmer and grimmer until Papa finally resigned March 25, 1931, at the bottom of the Depression.

The member who took the formal petition around for signatures was reported to have said. "Yes, it was me, I'm sorry to say; and I'd never do that again." But it was too late, the die was cast. I'm surprised Papa did not resign on his birthday, March 15. He used to quip that he was born on the day Caesar was warned about: "Beware the Ides of March."

Curious about the last few congregational meetings minutes of Pastor Belgum's tenure, I asked and received copies from a courteous parish secretary who sent me photocopies covering all seventeen years. But lo and behold! Pages 199 and 200 were missing, the very end of the story. Could Nixon have learned it from the Norwegians, the famous gap?

Since I taught Pastoral Theology for nine years in a seminary, I have been trying to put various pieces of Papa's troubled jigsaw puzzle together. Here are some speculations.

> 1. Papa was not strong on public relations, tact, and the "How to Win Friends and Influence People" model of administration. Rather it was a "Tell them the Truth and they can do what they want with it." Proclamation rather than persuasion or salesmanship.

> 2. Preaching and teaching in the Old Norwegian Synod was burdened with the heavy hand of fundamentalism and literalism. The Bible was inspired in every word and syllable, much like a teaspoon of medicine taken from any part of the bottle would have the same therapeutic effect. It was cast in stone in

antiquity. It is hard to make Scripture applicable and functional for modern daily life from this rigid perspective. But this was not just peculiar to Papa's personality, although it may have been congenial to his temperament; this was the stamp placed upon all graduates of the Norwegian Seminary in the first few decades of the century.

3. One contemporary of his said that quite a few members felt Papa was an intellectual and had missed his calling--he should have been a college professor. It is true he was a sharp linguist. At Luther College during one entire year of Latin he never got below 100% on any exam or exercise. This earned him the nickname of "Little Caesar." One said, "He spoke over the heads of people." I think his mannerism of looking somewhere above the back row and below the balcony was his way of not being distracted from his subject and its delivery. He was not interested in maintaining eye contact with his audience. This makes sense if the goal is simply to administer the Truth regardless of whether the medicine might be less than palatable.

4. Let us say the average pastor makes two mistakes and alienates two persons a month (not too bad); if he stays long enough he will have made the rounds of the whole parish. For example: One member was opposed to installing electricity in the church. At the dedication Papa said flat out, "And now maybe even Mr. ____ will be pleased with the electric lights." Dale Carnegie would never have advocated this approach. But then, he was a Methodist and not a Norwegian Lutheran Pastor.

5. Finally, it really does not matter, other than for academic curiosity, why Papa's ministry in this place came to an end, other than to show why it was a negative hassle, and what impact all of this might have had on my young life.

Interestingly, neither this negative phase nor its consequences deterred any of Papa's three sons from entering upon church work. Joe and I were both ordained and Harold for years worked for the Lutheran Welfare Society of Minnesota and for the national church body's Department of Parish Education. But then, remember how the grandparents dealt with adversity,

"... mostly you just took it on the chin, heaved an accepting sigh and went on with plowing, harvesting ..." and maybe in our case, church work. Church work doesn't stop because a few *Streels* are acting up on the prairie.

In later years I pondered what it might have meant to Papa, and other ministers of that era, when the parsonage wife was highly complimented, for example: "She is such a great help to him in his work; I don't see how he could do it without her." This is hardly Ego support and is not usually said of dentists, history professors, and other professionals. But just as a Catholic priest was forbidden to marry, among the Norwegian Lutherans, it was required of their clergy that they bring a "helpmate" who incidentally was qualified to play the organ, direct Christmas pageants, and otherwise do full-time church work for no wages. Today, as likely as not, the pastor's wife (or husband) has a well-paid career elsewhere.

Another concern I later had for clergy of that era was their penury and precarious financial status. Part of Papa's income was voluntary, free-will offerings at the three high festivals: Christmas, Easter, and Pentecost. If there was a fierce blizzard at Christmas, there went a chunk of Papa's income. I can still visualize the members marching around behind the altar, which was about three feet out from the back wall for this purpose, and depositing their offering in a plate as they emerged. Papa was supposed to stand facing the altar in all seriousness trying not to peek to see which one laid down a ten and which one a five. Just because a hair on the back of his head never twitched does not mean his eyeballs were not straining to see what kind of a grade he was being given by his many supervisors and employers.

Even at the young age of eight or so, I was slightly embarrassed when he would stop on the way home from a trip to Glenwood to see if the beekeeper had any misshapen combs, unsuitable for the market but good enough for the pastor. Such "gifts," or were they a form of relief for the underpaid minister, were also evident in the 10 percent discount given to clergy in those days in clothing stores, grocery stores and on the railroad listed as "clergy fare." There would also be a sack of oats for the horses from time to time.

I have wondered if the laity were evening the score. On the one hand the pastor had great authority to offer or withhold the Sacrament of the altar from an unrepentant member (The Office of the Keys). He had high status in the community; surely he did not need money on top of that. And we all know he is "called" to the ministry and not in it for money like merchants and farmers.

The hundredth anniversary booklet of the Barsness church shows three photos of the front of the church. In 1883 the pulpit was about five feet above the chancel floor; in the time Papa was there, the pulpit was about three steps up; and by 1937 the pulpit appears to be on the level of the chancel floor, only two steps above the main floor where the pews were. Wouldn't it be interesting to see if the salary went up as the status went down? Eric Berne could have listed it as one of the "Games People Play."

****

Excuse me for interrupting my story, but I must share an eye-opening experience I had this morning. You see, I decided to leave my comfortable home in Iowa City and take a run up to Glenwood and Starbuck, Minnesota, to check on my roots. Mrs. Matilda Barsness, the widow of Papa's successor, was willing to visit with me about the olden days. She also, most kindly, gathered a group of six elderly women and one man, who knew

Papa well and were now retired in Glenwood. They were full of stories of which the following are a good sample. I was privileged to take the group to lunch, and I thought I was attending an old-fashioned Ladies Aid meeting. Some items were news to me, others reinforced what I already suspected.

One Easter, a farmer failed to show up for worship, but, worse yet, missed his opportunity to contribute to the free-will offering which constituted part of Papa's annual income. Monday morning Papa stopped by this guy's farm and reminded him that he had missed out on his golden opportunity for Christian stewardship. He told the farmer that he could contribute a sack of grain for his turkeys. To which the man replied, "Well and good, I'll give you a sack of oats." Papa knew oats was not the most nutritious of grains and responded, "No, I want wheat," which he got. He suggested to another delinquent that he could clean out his barn in lieu of his contribution. He was flexible.

One Sunday as Papa was driving home from church, he met one of the Holtens approaching from the other direction, sitting on top of a load of hay. Papa, as was his style, admonished him for not being in church. The farmer replied (in Norwegian), "It is better to sit on the hay thinking about church than to sit in church thinking about the hay." Papa was up against a real philosopher.

Another salty response to the building project of jacking up the Barsness Church and putting a basement underneath complete with kitchen, for social gatherings and youth meetings, was this: "*Hvem skal leve der?*" (Who shall live there?)

Where does teaching leave off and criticism begin? When one person tries to "improve" another even with the best of intentions, it is often perceived as bad news. Even progress is bad news, because you are implying that I was <u>worse</u> before and should now be or do <u>better</u>. A comparative adjective is a tricky thing.

Cousin Herbert Belgum shared this typical example. Papa had strolled out to the field where Herb was plowing. Papa told him he was not plowing deep enough and proceeded to lower the plowshare two notches. As often happens, unsolicited advice results in no permanent change either of character or behavior. Herb told me that after he got over the hill and out of sight, he reset the plow where he wanted it. This trait may well be a congenital birth defect because I find myself doing the same thing. I guess we each gotta do what we gotta do.

A quote from one old Norwegian parishioner, one of Papa's friends and loyal supporters, was seconded by everyone present at the lunch: *"Han ser bare en höi plas i kroae"* (He looks only at a high place in the corner). (And, I, myself, observed that when he preached, he gazed above the heads of those in the back row and just below the balcony.)

Two ladies who could not attend the luncheon were kind enough to send me letters. One from Mrs. Inez Johnson is especially helpful since she quotes Papa directly. She and her mother, Ingeborg, had visited my folks when Papa was serving a church in Max, North Dakota.

> Pastor waxed very philosophical about his career as a pastor. He became a pastor because he promised his mother he would. In those early Scandinavian families it was a parental obligation to provide one son who would serve the Lord....
>
> Anton said he should never have been a pastor. He dreaded the delivery of sermons and never felt comfortable in the pulpit. He felt he was an inadequate speaker. He would have been much happier as a teacher or doing research.
>
> My impression of Anton was that he was a sincere servant of God and did his best to serve the parish. I recall he could not engage the parishioners with his eyes--he always looked over

our heads--I suspect this was the manifestation of his unease while delivering his sermon.

Sophie Vold Hauge shared these thoughts in her letter:

Confirmation brings up a memory of my first day of "reading for the minister" (confirmation class) as we always said then. I said, perhaps to myself, "Oh, I wish this was my last lesson instead of the first." After the session was over (was it three hours?) I said, perhaps again to myself, "I've changed my mind. This was great. In class we read a portion of the Acts of the Apostles." It meant so much because your father enjoyed it. He used no text--but he followed our reading with interest. I think he knew the book by heart. You could tell by the expression on his face that he loved that book….

You are interested in the events leading to your father's resignation. There was a special meeting at the Barsness Church. I recall your father standing before the assembled people and with great emotion he said that he had never preached anything but the Truth from the pulpit. It was such a sad moment.

Two things stand out in these accounts from his friends. First, he thought preaching was the central role of the pastor, and that preaching the Truth was the key requirement. Secondly, he really relished teaching and sensed that teaching should have been his vocation.

It was said by several that he was an intellectual and spoke over the heads of the people (substantively as well as visually). "He should have been a college professor." It is sometimes true that a public speaker, who is extremely well informed on his subject, takes for granted that his audience is also at home in that topic, hence leaves them behind in the dust.

If Papa had stayed a dozen years instead of seventeen, the pressure for his resignation may not have developed to the boiling point, and the following nine years of poverty and dislocation may not have taken place. Since this is a history, I may be forgiven for this insight in hindsight.

****

So what about me and my P-P-P-Pr-Pro-Problem? As well as I can reconstruct the scene, my stuttering started around the time when I began school at age five. I can remember with vivid exactness how mother instructed me to be polite and walk to school with my only classmate in the first grade, Marian Holten (whose family was part of the opposition and lived just north of the parsonage); but I was cautioned, "not to talk about anything we say in the house, because the Holtens might use it against Papa." Aha! That's about as good a definition of stuttering as I've come across: How to talk and not say anything.

My stuttering not only plagued me at school, but at Christmas programs in church and other times of public disgrace. The pastor's son could not only not speak the Word of God clearly, but hardly any other words as well. And he, the son of a linguist, "Little Caesar." I could almost hear the Ladies Aiders whispering, "Ja, it sure is too bad how it is vit him--and vat a burden for de Pastor and de Mrs. too you know."

Each class had to recite a poem with as many verses or lines as there were students in that group. Ours was an acrostic of STAR. Alphabetically, I was first up to bat. Holding up the gold "S" on a stick, I began my brief (or was supposed to have been brief) oration thus:

> "Ai-A-Aye-I'm Es-es-es S!
> Eb-eb-ehb-b-because I'm Shai-Shai-Shai-shining." (collapse)

First a tittering and giggling sounded like hail on a tin roof; then utter silence as many compassionate souls understood, "Hey, this ain't funny; this is pathetic. Get that poor kid out of there." But, of course, I had to stand there shamefacedly while more normal speakers whipped right through their lines:

> "I'm T because there is the star."
> "I'm A because aren't we happy it's Christmas."
> "I'm R because aren't you happy too?"

Not the best poetry, but then it was Christmas; and everyone should have a chance to say a piece.

Meanwhile, in the corner at the front was an enormous Christmas tree covered with real candles, a hundred or more, burning like crazy. A very large farmer stood on either side of the tree with a broom wrapped with a wet bath towel ready to touch the candle, which was kindling to the brittle branches, dried out by the hot-air furnace. When one sputtered, the watchman would tap it with a wet fire extinguisher and "Tsst" it was out. Once, before such a Christmas program, I had a vivid dream that the tree and the whole church caught fire, and the good news was that there didn't have to be any damn Christmas program that year.

Every parent wants a normal child; and it must be especially bothersome when the child lacks exactly what you cherish as a parent: The track coach with a lame son, the choirmaster with a tone deaf daughter, and the orator with a son who stutters. Persons who hope their child will learn quickly, and head in a straight beeline for college, want that child to be able to recite in class and "speak up" in class. Wendell Johnson, of speech pathology fame, once said that stuttering begins in the ear of the parent. "Say that again, more slowly this time." "O.K., just relax and say 'crocodile.' No, not 'eschlokadail'--like 'K' in Kaptain Krunch.' Alright, that's enough for now; we can always work on it again tomorrow." To which the inadequate speaker groaneth and travaileth until tomorrow--"may to-to-t-t-tah-tah-morrow ne-v-v-v-er kome. Hey! I just said 'k' like in klokadile."

It is amazing how quickly one's defect or stigma replaces one's given name like David, for example. On the school yard they are choosing up sides for a game. Finally, the last one is called. "Hey, Limpy, we're stuck with you. Get over here (you nothing person)." "Where's Fatso?" Even physically and mentally healthy persons can take it on the chin: "You're on our side, you Dumb Swede." Children can be very thorough and creative in denigrating a select few in the group to look down upon. And the victim has no defense since it is so true. He does limp, is overweight, Swedish by birth (although the dumb part may not be statistically accurate according to the normal curve), etc. Mimicking can be especially painful to behold because you are forced to see yourself as others see you, stuttering while you jerk your head, grimace your forehead, wobble your eyes, and otherwise look like a clown. To gain some acceptance I actually did start clowning around. It is such a weird game in a no-win situation.

It is easier to bear a deficiency if underneath there is a sure foundation of trust and security, such as I said characterized my early, pre-school years. But now, as Papa's position was becoming increasingly uncertain, the rumblings of the earthquake were reaching out from the epicenter to shake up significant others, of which I was definitely one. I suppose this is especially true of close families. If a victim of child abuse sees his father hauled off to jail, the reaction might well be, "I don't care--serves the old bastard right--good riddance." But here was Papa preaching the Truth and baptizing little children--doing what he'd always done--and the rug is pulled out from under him. And I'm supposed to protect him by "not talking about anything we say in the house, because the Holtens might use it against Papa." This was all backwards; the parents should protect the child. Only a psychoanalyst, after four years of careful digging, would be able to reveal the dynamics that went on in my young mind. We do know that in cases of divorce the child often assumes it is his/her fault.

True antagonists seek out ways of harassing the objects of their anger. The *Streels* even harassed me when my cousin and I were playing on a bank down by the creek, driving a little wind-up rubber tread caterpillar along roads we had carved out. They reported to the County Road Commission that the minister's son was destroying the road, the height of wanton vandalism. It would not be fruitful to continue this reminiscence of slights, injustice and persecution because both you and I would suspect I was exaggerating--maybe so. To whatever degree, it may be I have assumed that Papa's "Trouble" and my "Problem" were somehow eroding the foundation of my self-esteem.

To conclude this account of my early time of transition, the following photos are presented.

Marian, my "Companion" and Nemesis

The Little Boy in the Sailor Suit
Doesn't Have a Care in the World

What Became of the Happy, Carefree Boy in the Sailor Suit?

CHAPTER IV

STARBUCK = POVERTY

So what became of us when we moved out of the parsonage with no employment at the bottom of the Depression in 1931?

Papa assumed he should continue study of the Word of God even if he were not preaching it. He went back for a year of postgraduate study at the Norwegian Seminary in Saint Paul. Maybe with this added education he would receive a call to another parish somewhere. That happened in 1940.

Harold was away at Luther College in Iowa; so that left Mama, Joe, myself and one-year-old sister Dorothy to crowd in with our grandparents, Hans and Mari Johnshoy, on the north edge of Starbuck, ten miles to the west. We were fortunate to have this life raft. We furiously planted a three-acre garden (most of it in popcorn) on Grandpa's land. Mama canned a whole basement full of vegetables, rhubarb sauce, apples and meat (donated to us by farm relatives).

Joe and I shelled and popped corn for high school football and basketball games. In the summer months we set up our stand on Main Street. When a farmer with nine children would walk by, one of us would open the cover of the popper and "zing"--we had him in a cloud of delicious aroma. He had to buy enough popcorn for his family to bankrupt him. We knew it was unfair, but this was a matter of survival. At Christmas time Mama colored the popcorn with red and green syrup, and I peddled it for 25¢ for a large transparent cellophane bag.

Joe went on to become a great salesman of silos and sold enough in the summer to pay his way through the following year at college. I became one of the better Fuller Brush salesmen in the area. I even sold hairbrushes to the bald-headed men insisting that the genuine Chinese boar bristles were excellent for scalp massage. I also sold shower bath brush outfits to farmers with no running water. I "taught" them how to rig up a platform of boards behind the barn, hang a pail full of warm water from a nail in the barn wall, and voila, there's your shower bath. "You farmers, working in the dusty harvest, deserve a Fuller Shower Bath Brush Set more than the city slickers in town. That will be $6.95 please."

As you can see, poverty can be rather character building. I believe Joe and I both felt the same way toward preaching, that it was our job to "sell" useful ideas to the people; and I always felt that way later in life as a professor. What good is an idea, insight or theory if no one buys it?

When Papa returned after more learning, but no closer to a call, Uncle Herman Johnshoy, who had been successful as a politician in the capital, Saint Paul, wangled a job for Papa as Assistant Postmaster in Starbuck, which did not have quite enough business for one person, let alone two. We moved into the "Sando House," and Grandpa's and Grandma's life could return to normal--not that we gave up the enormous, lifesaving garden the entire six years we lived in Starbuck. When the Harvest Festival came to town, we always provided the carnies and sideshow folks with vegetables and also peddled some of them around town.

Next came the experience of "being on relief" together with the millions and millions of other Americans who were grateful to F.D.R.'s "New Deal" with W.P.A. (Works Progress Administration), C.C.C. (Civilian Conservation Corps), N.Y.A. (National Youth Administration), on and on, with other acronyms that kept folks from starvation and homelessness. But in our family it had also a sad twist. Here was Papa, Pastor A.H. Belgum, faithfully digging a trench for the new sewer system in town alongside other unemployed men. It meant that Uncle

Casper Johnshoy, not my father, would confirm me. It must have taken a psychological toll on all of us that we were not aware of at the time--protected by Norse fatalism, "It was meant to be." Meanwhile, many wealthy speculators had solved their economic problems by jumping out of Wall Street skyscraper windows. Recently, when our Iowa farmers spoke about the "Farm Crisis," I knew exactly what they meant. Although survivors found ways of coping, poverty was really never that much fun.

Seeking ever cheaper housing, we finally ended up at the bottom of the heap in the "Oleson House" at the extreme southeast corner of the village just before the swamp tapers off into Lake Minnewaska. Elmer Oleson, who was a bachelor and tended the stockyard stalls down by the railroad tracks, lived in one of the rooms upstairs. The aroma of his room was quaint to say the least. He was a self-educated man about fifty years of age, who corresponded widely to add to his considerable stamp collection. He was glad to show it off and explain the triangular and colorful shapes from Africa and the Far East; and he also helped me to start my own stamp collection. Back when radios were coming into their own, he had a crystal set, which could pick up foreign signals. He maybe heard more first-hand reports on Hitler's growing reputation than anyone else in town, getting information from England, Norway, etc.

Speaking of radios, we had a small, brown plastic Emerson that worked quite well. If I finished my chores after school, I could listen to "Jack Armstrong, the All-American Boy" and "The Adventures of Little Orphan Annie" and her millionaire Daddy Warbucks. If you sent in certain coupons from Wheaties or Ovaltine containers, you could receive in the mail your very own decoder ring or map of the "Lost Mine" with the treasure still very likely buried there. And you'd be the first to know the secret and report the next day at school, stuttering or no stuttering.

You guessed it, I entered into adolescence, otherwise known as puberty, "baas," "fishda" and like that.

I recall during one summer vacation, sitting too close to a girl my age. She smelled strange to say the least--somewhere between Lysol and a very strong laundry detergent, maybe medicine of some kind--but she didn't really look sick. It would be years before I realized that she was experiencing what a TV ad has politely called "difficult days."

I did not get any of what is now euphemistically called "family life education" (a term used to get it by some school boards). The closest I came was the time Mama asked Harold (back from college) "to have a talk" with me. He told me two things as briefly as possible. They can be summed up as "Don't play with yourself" (I wondered if that included marbles and solitaire); and "You can't be too careful." I remember my assuring him I'd be careful about whatever it was I was supposed to be careful about (but I fell out of a bag swing anyway). It reminded me of the minister who was asked to give a talk about sex to Lions' Club. Embarrassed, he answered his wife's query by telling her he would be talking about "Sailing." The Lions' wives commented at the next morning coffee time how their husbands had found the talk most helpful. She replied, "I don't know why he is such an expert on that; he's only done it twice, once he lost his hat, and the other time he almost fell out of the boat." No wonder one of the books I wrote later in my career was *The Church and Sex Education.*

Farm kids are more knowledgeable about sex. They even know how to make it impossible for male pigs to become fathers of baby pigs. On a visit to one farm a boy my age showed me how to masturbate. I thought it was quite remarkable. Now, of course, every young person discovers something about sexuality one way or another, fortunately before they get married, whether from the football coach in a "Hygiene" class in the 11th grade or by accident, like becoming P.O.W. (Pregnant Out of Wedlock).

Unfortunately, a person with low self-esteem may latch onto instant gratification when routine achievements or socialization are not sufficient to make oneself feel good (a life full of football, socializing, dances, friends etc.). In other words, something that may not be a big deal in and of itself becomes disproportionately important, somewhat distorted. This happens when a glass of beer becomes more than a nice beverage to go with a steak dinner. Thus, a salesman, who has fallen way below his quota on the first leg of his trip, arrives at his hotel so down that he says to himself, "I'm entitled to a little happiness in life." Sure enough, 4-5 Manhattans or Martinis provides him with "a little happiness in life." I'm afraid masturbation became disproportionately useful to me in this way.

Later in a college Abnormal Psychology course, I learned about the syndrome called "obsessive compulsive behavior." Alcoholism and over-eating are obviously in this category; so are thumb sucking and fingernail biting, and, you guessed it, stuttering. Yes, it is clear to me that, even though I no longer have a problem with stuttering, I am a compulsive talker. One graduate student gave me a complimentary evaluation but added, "Professor Belgum tends to keep on talking after the point is made." He was right on target. I have quipped that I still have spasms, but they come out in paragraphs and sometimes last for fifty minutes (the length of a class lecture).

I should not leave the impression that everything in the Starbuck era was gloom and doom. Playing my saxophone in the band and getting to go to the State Music Contest in Minneapolis was a high point. We played in the enormous, 4,000-seat

Northrup Auditorium on the university campus. Sleeping
overnight way up on the fifth floor of the old West Hotel in the
Minneapolis Loop was a thrill. Also, my friend, Jim Moen, and I
developed a 4-H Club demonstration of how to plant, transplant
and pack tomatoes for the market, which went over so well at the
Pope County Fair that we got to attend the Minnesota State Fair,
all expenses paid, for a week. Sleeping under the open
grandstand and hearing the race cars rev up their motors for
practice runs early in the morning is still vivid in my memory.
And, of course, my faithful dog, "Bugs," understood and liked
me.

CHAPTER V

BLESSING OF DEPERSONALIZATION

For me, leaving the warm, tightly knit society of Starbuck for the big city was truly emancipating. In a small town everything is magnified, your achievements and your handicaps. You tend to be pegged as this or that and remain in that category, or so it seemed to me as far as my stuttering was concerned and as far as Papa's loss of status and station in life was concerned.

We moved to Minneapolis in the middle of my tenth grade year, about Christmas, 1937. The Depression was still in full swing. Uncle Herman had come to the rescue and had found for Papa a custodian's job in the Department of Rural Credit located on the city limits between Minneapolis and Saint Paul on University Avenue. Once again we were indebted to political patronage, Herman's connections in state government. At fifty-six years of age, Papa was grateful to be able to support his family again without being on relief.

Brother Joe and I would go with Papa on the weekends to help with mopping the floors and the general heavy work that came once a week. We were glad to pitch in. Although Papa was in good health, we tended to think of him now as "older."

The very nice five-room apartment we moved into at 215 Melbourne Avenue was only a short walk to Papa's work, so no need for a car. It was a great location with the land behind our apartment falling away to Franklin Avenue and the Mississippi River and the River Road parkway. Just across the side street on our same Melbourne Avenue lived Dr. Owen Wangensteen in a grand brick home. He was a famous surgery professor at the University of Minnesota's Medical School; so, as Mother said, "You see we are not for the cat." How we had come up in the

53

world! Dorothy had only a couple blocks to walk to Sidney Pratt
Elementary School. And continuing up a steep hill we could
climb to the water tower on the crown of Prospect Park Hill,
from where you could see miles in any direction. What a grand
level to which we had been promoted, a situation I would not
have dreamed of as a dweller in the Oleson House in Starbuck.

My walk to John Marshall High School, named after the
great U.S. Supreme Court Justice, was an easy mile's walk down
University Avenue past the fraternity houses or sometimes
through the campus. Everything was new and interesting to me.
Marshall High was an ideal situation for me in my personality
development. It was impressive, occupying a full city block with
eighteen hundred students (7th through 12th grade).

I enjoyed getting lost in the crowd. All these students were
too busy rushing around to zero in on me to see when I would
have my next spasm. In retrospect I would call it one of the
blessings of depersonalization. Nor were the students at all
concerned about the vocation or status of each other's parents.
For example, it was a couple years before I realized that the
father of one of my lunch buddies was Dean of the Institute of
Technology and an eminent engineer, nor was it ever mentioned
that Elizabeth Bird's father was the well known Professor of
Social Psychology. It did not give one a personal leg up that
one's parents were from high in the industrial or business ranks
of society. This was paradise, a truly egalitarian society where
each one operated and achieved in his/her own right, not by
"connections." I may have been naive, but that is what it seemed
like to me; and it felt good.

I was delighted and felt privileged to play my little B-flat
soprano saxophone in the marching band and strutted proudly in
the Minneapolis Aquatennial Parade while my closest friend,
David Boxrud, tossed his baton high over the streetcar wires and

caught it to the applause of the crowd. I almost stopped long enough to shout, "Hey, he's my friend." The gold braid on my cap, the bright red jacket and white trousers with a gold braid down the outside would have raised the self esteem of the humblest Norwegian Lutheran. I was having no trouble with "thought, word and deed" that day; that's for sure! By the way, David Boxrud stuttered too, as did Mr. Belstrom, the band director. No matter, as long as we got the job done.

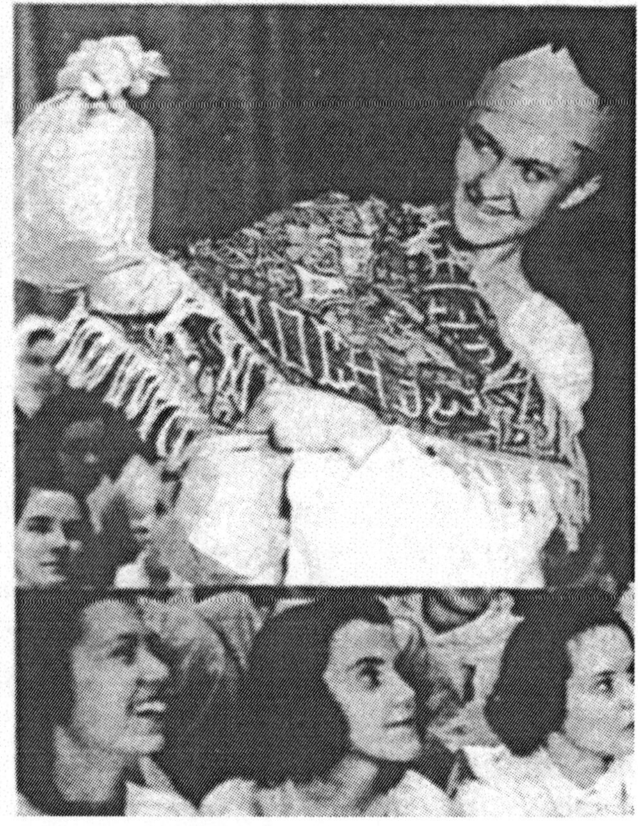

King Midas with bags of Gold in Latin Club Play
Below: A few admiring students

Marshall High had so many severely handicapped students that I soon saw my speech impediment in a new light. Buses with special lifts brought kids with polio, cerebral palsy, epilepsy and much more from all over Minneapolis. We were a special education center. One I remember had such weak hand bones that a leather binding held them together; yet he wheeled his own wheelchair down the hall and somehow banged through the classroom door at Marshall, and no one did for such students what they could do on their own. This fellow also played clarinet in the orchestra.

Louis Henderson, totally blind since birth, played the violin in the orchestra and did so very well. He also managed to walk onto the stage and find his own seat in the first violin section without knocking anything over at concert time. He could take notes in class with the Braille method as fast as the rest of us could write. He seemed very well adjusted indeed. He went on to the university where he was an outstanding scholar and then committed suicide. It shook us deeply.

When you associate very naturally and comfortably with the clarinetist, the violinist, the halt and the maimed, the deaf and those in the "sight saving class" at lunch or in the hallways, at the parties and attending games, you slow down your own complaining by at least eighty percent. Abnormal people seemed almost normal at Marshall High. It was a form of grace and acceptance I had not experienced before in such a wholehearted manner. I credit our teachers for being exceptional role models. Yes, I was glad to be in this institution of a school, depersonalized in some ways as any mob scene is, yet remarkably supportive just because you were you. You didn't have to be SOMEBODY to be somebody.

The church we attended, University Lutheran Church of Hope, was also large, considerably larger than the town of

Starbuck. In retrospect I am puzzled why I had the gall to enter a church oratorical contest. No one tittered or giggled like hail on a tin roof. Everything went on schedule, "Next please." I can't even remember what it felt like. It was just another event, I guess, certainly not a federal case. No one asked why Papa did not have a call or why he was a janitor. We felt right at home.

It was from this church I went to Summer Bible Camp about a hundred miles west of Minneapolis, near Willmar. Another positive experience, socializing, making friends, even a stray date growing out of these friendships. Life was going along very well on many fronts.

By the way, my grades at Marshall were considerably better than in Starbuck even in such courses as Botany, Geometry, Latin and Social Studies. It all hangs together, doesn't it; peace of mind, self regard, grades, socialization and attitude. Yet, for me, it all came together in the big city amidst the depersonalization of crowded halls and milling traffic, where people were not so interested in whether you were Lutheran, Norwegian, the Pastor's son and on and on, as they were about the functions you fulfilled, the role you played whether in band, class, laboratory or extracurricular activities.

Years later, I wrote a little paperback book for Concordia Publishing House on how to live in our increasingly depersonalized society with its Social Security numbers, categories, policy and procedure manuals, the works. It was called *Alone, Alone, All All Alone.*

Working Like A Man came toward the end of high school. I got this job at the Farm Campus, site of the Colleges of Forestry, Agriculture and Home Economics of the University of Minnesota in the northwest edge of Saint Paul. Plus about twenty buildings for classes and laboratories, there were another seven hundred or so acres of experimental crop and pasture land, barns for cattle, hogs, horses, poultry, etc. The crew I was on dealt with the grounds, landscaping and maintaining the lawns and flower beds, watering and mowing and trimming.

The superintendent, L.B. Basset, was a good instructor and disciplinarian, setting an example of concern for excellence. Four of us had one fourth of the campus each for which we were responsible. He would say, "If you need more sprinklers, just ask me; but you must keep it green all summer." In my quadrant, among other things, was a lawn which was two blocks long and a block wide with every kind of bush, shrub and tree that would grow in Minnesota planted around the three sides of this area. It was the hands-on lab for the Forestry students. I took great pride in maintaining it as well as trimming around the Ag Engineering, Dairy and Administration buildings. It was a positive experience in real work.

One day I was assigned to accompany Randy, who was a tough, swearing he-man, to gather in the field corn from a certain field. He was brown and sweating and smoked a cigar. He drove the team of horses between two rows of corn bundles between six and seven feet long. They were heavy. I'd throw the bundles onto the hay rack and he would do the same on his side. This went on all day. It is not the simple facts of this task that I want to share; it was the meaning it held for me at the end of the day. I reflected that I had hoisted exactly as many pounds or tons of the stuff as Randy had. Since everybody knew he was a real he-man, obviously I must be one too. We were equals. Oh, I realized he was thirty-five and I was seventeen; he had a family and I was single, but I mean in terms of work accomplished on that day, we were equals. It was one of those "Aha!" experiences when a new insight dawns, a new self-awareness. I changed my self-concept and promoted myself to full-fledged manhood. It was a great feeling.

Keeping my section of the campus as perfectly neat as possible also gave me great satisfaction. No amount of counseling to help me feel a sense of worth or self-esteem would have meant to me what experiencing the pride of seeing the results of my work did. No one had to tell me I had done a good job; I could see it for myself. That is especially significant for us Norwegians, who claim to put ourselves down but actually beg for compliments in subtle ways. "It's too bad how the cake fell together." "Oh, no! Olga this cake is outstanding." Or, among the farmers: "It isn't much for a farm, but maybe if I work at it, it can amount to something." "But, Lars, the elevator man told me you got the most bushels to the acre of wheat of anyone around. You sure have a good farm."

I have caught myself, after having spoken to a group, asking the program chairperson if he thought it was a good turnout only to be told that usually they have a larger attendance at the meetings. "How do you think the discussion afterwards went?" trying again. "Well, we usually have many more questions, but then, it was OK." It reminds one of the bishop who asked the local minister about the small crowd, saying, "Didn't they know the Bishop was coming to speak?" "Yes," his host replied. "Word leaked out." For some of us it is a constant task of re-inventing the wheel as we go around: work-worth-work-worth, sometimes showing remarkable maturity and ego integrity and then slipping back into our old insecurities and begging for support. That experience with the corn bundles and Randy is one I like to reflect on from time to time.

Some years later a new perspective came into focus. I am worthy because God has declared me his child in baptism. Hence, I am entitled to work. I don't have to work to become worthy. There are so many angles to this question of worth, self-worth and self-esteem. I've wrestled with it for seventy years.

Just last spring, I published an article entitled "Guilt and/or Self-Esteem as Consequences of Religion." It is the first time I've received so many requests for reprints--from seven countries plus a variety of American universities and psychotherapists. Evidently, it is a problem common for many beside myself.

Mama had the idea that we could rent a large house right near the campus and take in student roomers to add to the family income. That we did by moving to 506 Oak Street. This was not as elegant but economically practical. This worked fine for about a year and then a great opening came up for Papa. He received a call to a rural parish near Green Bay, Wisconsin. It was called Green Valley. The long depression, at least as far as Papa's pastoral vocation was concerned, was over. He was back in the pulpit where he belonged. The family photo from this era shows a contented and secure family that had weathered the storm and was on course again.

David in the Middle
Between the Scholar and the Athlete
With Sister Dorothy about Eight Years Younger than I
Papa and Mama glad to be back in the parsonage

CHAPTER VI

FREE AT LAST

The last thing Mama did before leaving for the Green Valley parsonage was to leave me a small inheritance. In exchange for the bedding and rooming-house furniture, the couple who took over 506 Oak Street were to give me board and room for my first year at the University of Minnesota. The new lady of the house was an ardent Christian Scientist, and thereby hangs a tale.

One washday she missed her step on the uneven basement floor and totally sprained her ankle. It swelled up like a football, but, of course, she paid it no never mind since there is no such thing as disease, injury or pain. They are all illusions of erroneous thinking, heresies. Even matter does not really exist. All is truth, light and beauty. There could hardly have been spelled out a doctrine more exactly opposite to the one on which I was reared: Original Sin, the Old Adam and the evils that lurk in "thought, word and deed," to say nothing of the "sins of the flesh." Oh yes, definitely the FLESH exists and is largely "baas" and "fishda." If I would have asked her if her ankle hurt, she would have replied, "What ankle? I don't see any ankle around here." She walked it out without a slight evidence of pain. Remarkable! I would have much to learn in my new life.

The new roommate I inherited in the transaction was another interesting case. He was a handsome, black-haired, tall Norwegian from up country, and a drama major. He was marvelous in the lead role of *Peer Gynt,* the first University Theater play I attended. But he was not much of a role model as far as being a student was concerned. He could not register for any class before noon, because that was when he got up. It was the routine of the theater crowd and other artsy students to stay up late. There would be play practice all evening and then carousing until the wee hours. Then up and at'em for a literary criticism or problems of style class at two or three in the afternoon. I never went out with him on those rendezvous, but somehow it disoriented what should have been an orderly life for me. My grades were miserable and I flunked Greek, which I had no business taking my first term anyway. Oh, well, it got better.

Yes, it got better when I hooked up with the ideal roommate for me, another Norwegian Lutheran pastor's son, Jim Tetlie. He got all A's. What was his secret? Eight hours of sleep a night. No matter if a bull session was under way, when 11:00 p.m. came around, he got out of his chair and into his bed. I decided to imitate him. He rose promptly at 7:00 a.m. sharp and alert. He also was exceedingly well self-disciplined. Moral of the story for me was: Find a winner and imitate him. I began making A's too.

Jim also had single-mindedness. His goal was to be an eye-ear-nose-and-throat doctor. When he was a very small boy, a kind Dr. Hilding in Duluth, Minnesota, took care of his adenoids. As he looked up at the wonderful man, he decided to imitate him and become like him. If that meant going to college and then medical school, that was OK with him, anything to be like Dr. Hilding. He never had any problem registering for courses. He just said, "Give me anything that will lead to being an eye-ear-nose-and-throat doctor." In the Army he did precisely this kind of work and, when discharged, what else, went back to Duluth and became a junior partner with Dr. Hilding with little kids looking admiringly into his honest and kind face.

My route was not so direct and focused. I dabbled and was interested in everything. Each course became a possible vocation. Zoology was the most amazing and earth rattling, to say nothing of doctrine rattling, for me. Here I was like a crustacean parsonage kid with the intellectual framework on the outside holding me together.   Actually, humans are supposed to have the skeleton on the inside, with a lot of inner support and a stiff spine to hold them up. Yes, what I was brought up on was a rigid structure of fundamentalist, literalist interpretation of the universe and my place in it. Here, Zoology 101, Dr. Dawson was throwing out a new doctrine, scientific, experimental, inductive method of thinking. Study the data and see where they lead. Don't come to a question with preconceived ideas. Oh, no! Where will this roller coaster lead us? Paddle a canoe like this and you could go right over Niagara Falls or to Hell in a basket.

Professor Dawson was a follower of the Anti-Christ, Darwin, and preached his heresy, "Evolution." Each year he would be challenged by the pastor of the big, downtown First Baptist Church to a public debate on evolution vs. what he called "Bible Creationism." He had as his main supporting evidence the chronological data at the top of the first page of the Bible popular in that day. It indicated that the creation of nature and man took place at a much later date than the "landform evolution" theory of Leonardo da Vinci, Agricola and others in the sixteenth century. The *Britannica* explains it thus: "… Archbishop Ussher of Ireland, for example, concluded from biblical studies in 1654 that earth and man had been created in 4004 BC, on October 26 at 9:00 a.m." Although the poor minister always made a fool of himself, his supporters cheered him on for his bravery in taking on the "godless University and its infidels." It was an unfortunate warfare between town and gown, between science and religion.

Professor Dawson was not above a little shady lecturing on some points. Once he showed slides of children's necks swollen with horrid parasites. It was pitiful. Then he explained how biological research required use of experimental animals. But the

Anti-vivisection League was against helping these poor little children. And who was their current president? None other than ("next slide please") the Episcopal Bishop of Massachusetts. Moral of the story unspoken but very clear: Science cares about little children; religionists care more about animals. Yes, you guessed it; Professor Dawson was the rebellious and disillusioned son of a clergyman. So, even though I realized now that science was also not 100 percent objective, the growing evidence of biological evolution threw me into the toils.

About three blocks from the Zoology Building was Grace University Lutheran Church where C.A. Wendell was pastor. He had an M.A. in Biology and had worked out his own reconciliation between science and religion, between the facts of science and the poetry and dramatic interpretations of reality we find in Scripture. They were both describing the same thing from different perspectives, with different styles of language. He was an enormous help to me in coming to grips and finding peace in the matter. Today even the King James version of the Bible does not have Bishop Ussher's dating at the top of each page.

The Lutheran Students Association was a very significant support to me in my transition from a conservative to a liberal and liberating theology. The able campus pastor was Carl E. Lund-Quist, who was as at home with the Dean of Students and Faculty eating lunch in the prestigious Faculty Club on the top floor of the Union as he was with the students of every temperament and intellectual level. The L.S.A. was the largest student organization on campus, and key student leaders were also to be found at the Sunday evening meetings in the Great Hall of the YMCA. We would have a cheap macaroni and cheese supper or some other menu that could be thrown together for $.25. The visiting was great. This was followed by an outstanding speaker on some exciting topic, usually someone who was equally respected in academic as well as church circles. Then, by the time I was a junior, came my chance to shine as the community song leader. I can assure you I was fabulous. This was a time when actions accompanied songs such as "Down By the Old Mill Stream," "Do Your Ears Hang Low," etc. I would slow them down from rowdy to sentimental and finally some spirituals. There were social mixers and games and just plain fun. It suited me to a "T."

You may wonder how I handled the depersonalization of this vast University of 15,000. In registering, for example, I just got there quite early and was twelfth in line. The friendly registrar took care of me in no time at all. Although there were six hundred in all in the history lecture course and there were too many to bother with taking attendance, I sat in the front row and looked upon it as a very intimate relationship with no one between me and my professor. Professor Elliott, the Head of the Psychology Department, listed two office hours per week. Since everyone thought he would be far too busy to see anyone, no one came, and I could see him whenever I wanted since his office was usually empty of students. Getting my major advisor to sign a slip changing my major could have been a bureaucratic night-mare as many students found; but since I waited till he was headed for lunch with his hat and coat on and approached him in a nice Dale Carnegie manner in the hall, he gladly signed whatever I handed him. Radar in the MASH program learned it from me. To me the University of Minnesota was just another small, friendly school.

A strange thing happened to me academically. You recall my telling you that Papa drilled me on grammar even before I began school. Well, I never had any patience with high school English with its twenty-seven rules for punctuation and this and that. So when I took the College English Placement Test, I did so badly on the mechanics and rules part that I was placed in what was euphemistically called "Bonehead English," officially, "Subfreshman English," which dummies had to take before beginning with real freshman English, a required course. I sloshed through this stuff enough to get out of the woods. But then, in my junior year, I thought that if I am that poor in English I'd better sign up for Advanced Composition, Problems of Style and Short Story Writing. In all of these I got straight A's because the professors did not want to know if you knew the logistics of linguistics, but simply whether you could write clearly and interestingly.

I was admitted to the honorary writing fraternity, Delta Phi Lambda, and got my first article published. I named it "S-S-S-Stuttering." It was accepted by *Hygeia* magazine, the American Medical Association's lay periodical found in physicians' waiting rooms. I got a handsome $15 for my effort. Later in the year I got another check from *Science Digest,* which had re-issued it. They sent me $25. That was when tuition was $20 a quarter. I was also happy to have my term paper for Professor Elliott's Psychology class published in *The Lutheran Outlook,* "Personality Portrait of Luther." So things went fairly well academically and I received my B.A. in June of 1944.

I must back up and share with you the most important part of my years at the University of Minnesota, the Speech Clinic (two hours every afternoon for two years). My mother had set up an appointment for me to meet Dr. Bryng Bryngelson, Director of the Speech Clinic, about whom she had heard, I believe, on a radio program. This was the summer after high school. I promptly forgot all about it, evidently not ready yet to consider myself a "client." Although I had made considerable adjustment in life through the Marshall High School years, stuttering was still too prominent a part of my equipment for my own good. One useful way of cutting down on the pain of stigma is to deny it or repress it down into the cellar of the psyche. It doesn't go away, but out of sight, out of mind, or so some of us think.

When I registered as a freshman, I was somehow ready to deal with the Speech Clinic and whatever they might decide to throw at me in terms of "treatment." It was located on the fourth floor of Folwell Hall, a long and impressive structure right on University Avenue at the entrance to the campus, where the Inter-Campus street car made its loop. Those of us who climbed those wide stairs and steadied ourselves on the massive banister were an artful group of dodgers. One victim said his father wanted him to have "breathing lessons." If he breathed correctly he would talk better. Another, in a fit of self-disclosure, popped his glass eye out of its socket and rapped it on the table and exclaimed, "Ah-a-nd th-ah th-ah that's an-n-n-naugh-another thing Ia-Ia- I'm ashamed of, y-y-you know; but I d-d-do have a gl-gl-glass eye." It was dramatic because from that moment on he did not need to hold his left hand over his eye, rub his eye, hide his eye, do all kinds of gymnastics so as to pretend there was nothing wrong with his eye. He had grasped the first principle of the Clinic: Be honest and admit who you are. And key for all of us was to admit we were stutterers and quit pretending, hiding, avoiding, postponing and using another dozen gimmicks we had developed to deal with our "non-problem." A few decades later, the phrase was, "Let it all hang out."

I did not know at the time how fortunate I was to be enrolling at the University of Minnesota where one of the four pioneering, premier speech clinics was available. The other three were Western Michigan at Kalamazoo, University of Wisconsin in Madison and the University of Iowa in Iowa City. I came to know that several speech pathologists stuttered and had come to this vocation out of personal search for help. Wendell Johnson at Iowa was one such. His M.A. thesis was entitled *Because I Stutter*. He wrote, "I decided to specialize in my own ordeal."

Dr. Bryng Bryngelson was an enormous help to me; and I also took his course, "Personality Development Through Speech." Ironically, he was a disenchanted son of a Swedish Covenant minister and figured religion caused more problems than it solved. Yet it was under his tutelage and the work of his staff that I came to accept myself. Paul Tillich defined grace as "Loving the unlovely and accepting the unacceptable." Lutherans claim over and over again that their central doctrine is "saved by grace." But I never experienced it being acted out in Barsness or Starbuck in the church, as such, or in the community among the "communion of saints." I had to learn it from, of all people, a Swede, and one who had lapsed from the church at that. I was greatly indebted to Bryngelson for helping me turn my life completely around.

The treatment made perfect sense once you got the hang of it. I recall sitting in front of a very large, full-length mirror beside my therapist. I could see her in the mirror, but I was supposed to focus on myself when speaking to her. In other words, I would see myself as others see me. I would also see what I was really doing: jerking my head around, wrinkling up my forehead, twitching and squirming. One fellow used to hit his hip to pop out a word. It quickly dawned upon me that hardly any of these "secondary symptoms," as they called them, had anything whatsoever to do with the speech mechanism. They were actually efforts to avoid stuttering: to jerk the sound out, to force the word out, to do something drastic so we could get on with the rest of the sentence.

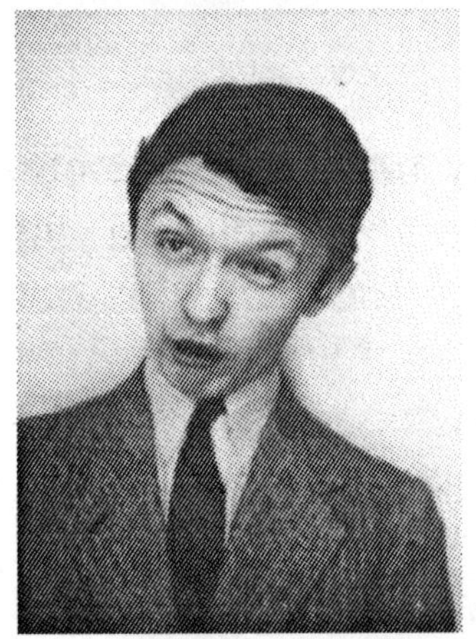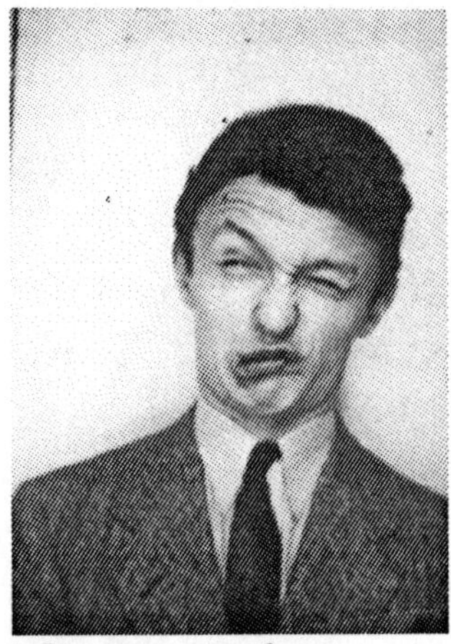

Many people think that stuttering
is not all that attractive.

The photo above was taken at the University of Minnesota Speech Clinic, but is no exaggeration. I compensated by clowning around, but it was a cover-up for my inner sense of inferiority and shame over my defective speech. A descriptive word check list to characterize me in the pre-adolescent childhood would include, among others:

Poverty	Not too bright	Shame
Weak	Lonely	Self-doubt
Fat	Insecure	Vandalism
Spasms	Inferiority feelings	Devious

It was not a pretty picture. These are words that come to mind as I free-associated about my childhood in Starbuck. It is little wonder I hardly ever went back there. About 25 or 30 years later I was invited back to preach at the 90th anniversary of the church in Starbuck. Mostly, the people who remembered me were amazed I could talk, and commented on it at length. Instead of complimenting me on the great healing the Speech Clinic had wrought in my life, they focused on "Boy, oh boy, how you used to stutter." "Yah, you could hardly say anything without stuttering; I remember that." If I'm invited back for the 125th anniversary, someone will say, "My father is in the nursing home, but he asked me to listen closely and see if you still stutter."

Actually, if there is a shortage somewhere in our wiring, some nerve synapse that doesn't close quickly, or whatever, that would be as short a stoppage as flicking off and on a light switch, hardly n-oticeable in ordinary s-peech. It is getting all psyched up about it, getting into a stew or panic that causes all the splashing around, the fireworks and gymnastics. That's how hard we were trying not to stutter and it wasn't helping at all.

Maybe if we played our cards right no one would "N#//!ooot*+T-t-t-tT-T#ice we were having a s-Sss-s-puh-puh$&//-asm." That is a stutterer's shorthand for saying "notice we were having a spasm." So what should we do about it?

First, we had to become aware of spasms when they occurred. We took a note pad to the dinner table, and, as we were talking, would make a mark to record a spasm had arrived. This helped us become aware of what was happening inside ourselves during speech. Secondly, it provided an opportunity for "advertising" to our table mate that we were going (Oh, shucks, yes) to the Speech Clinic to work on our stuttering.

A neurological puzzle is this. Why would I clutch up introducing myself to a girl at the Lutheran Student Association supper? Because I knew the "B" word, Belgum, would have to be conquered somehow (Should I pole vault over it, or ram through it, run around it, knock it down, kick it like a football, or just give up and go home?). Yet, I could sing in the choir the anthem "Beautiful Savior" with no problem at all with the letter "B." Also, I could read a poem in unison with a dozen other students and have no trouble with "b" in banana, boy or bedbug. Even more fanciful is the fact that a stutterer can perform the role of a character in a play and not stutter on the dreaded "b" because

Robin Hood does not stutter. What goes on in the sneaky psyche we can only guess.

Some of our "advertising" assignments were pretty grotesque. A fellow clinic mate (going in pairs so we could not cheat) and I once had to board the Como Harriet street car near campus and ride to Fifth Street. From the front of the car one of us would shout a question to the conductor stationed at the fare box in the rear. "H-h-h-how d-d-d-o I-I-I t-t-t-transfer t-t-t-to S-S-S- Saint P-P-Paul?" A spasm on every word whether one came naturally or not. The point of the assignment was that all the startled passengers and disgusted conductor should know who we were--weird, abnormal, shamefully defective freaks who stuttered. So there! What we discovered after we had wiped up the floor and departed for our boarding club for supper was that, contrary to our fears, the end of the world had not come. We were still alive, and, after a night's sleep, would go to class and Clinic tomorrow. So what if others discover you are a bit deviant. They can do what they want with it: laugh, cry, turn away, snicker, even titter and giggle like hail on a tin roof. We were just fed up with waiting to find out if everyone else had decided whether we were worthy folks or were entitled to a little self-esteem. These exercises were crash courses in this realization. Once we learned the lesson, we did not have to repeat it *ad nauseam.* Oh, what a relief!

By the way, the last year at the University I actually had a job as conductor on that Como Harriet streetcar. A couple years ago I wrote a short story, "The 5:08," which is also the title of the collection, published privately. It describes the agony for the stuttering conductor announcing the streets: "when he got through with Baa-Baa-Bancroft, one couldn't help but finish the line with 'have you any wool?'"

"Bouncing" was another device for structuring our speech. You can tell when a spasm is coming on, now that you've become more self aware and are not defending yourself from reality. Of course there will be a short stoppage (st-oppage). For good measure let's make two more stoppages, in other words when you have a spasm, bounce three times (t-t-t-imes) and then proceed with the rest of the word (imes). Then, with practice, we were able to leave off the extra superfluous two bounces and let it go at the one bounce, a basic spasm (t-imes). By this time we have already forsaken the devious devices we had relied on to keep from stuttering, to blast through if necessary, to jerk it out like pulling a calf that won't cooperate in the birth process, etc. Why go through all that fuss since you don't care if they find out you stutter anyway?

The lessons I learned at the Speech Clinic went far beyond stuttering. It was about honesty and not counting on hypocrisy to get you out of a tight spot. The principles applied to many other handicaps and conditions about which shame is associated. At the University Hospital in Iowa City, I later developed a course on "Stigma" and wrote a paperback, *WHAT CAN I DO ABOUT THE PART OF ME I DON'T LIKE?* And I was asked to speak about this to numerous groups. You can see why I am so indebted to my Alma Mater and my heretical helper, Bryng Bryngelson. I was free at last!

You can understand why for a while I seriously considered majoring in speech pathology and passing on the blessing I had received to others. But I thought there were more problems that could be addressed through psychiatry, wider field of service. Once I calculated how much math and chemistry I would have to master, to say nothing of learning the Latin names for all four sides of every bone in the human body and which tendons and ligaments they connect to, all that to get through medical school

so I could begin studying psychiatry … NO SIR! One advantage
of humility is that you do not tend to overreach yourself.
Remember how I said I took Greek as a freshman. I had
theological seminary in mind then and thought I would use Greek,
which was required at the Norwegian Seminary, as my foreign
language requirement in college. I now returned to that
vocational goal. After all, pastoral care and counseling can also
help many distressed and distorted and fearful folks, as the
Episcopal Prayer Book says, "all sorts and conditions."

In 1940, as I entered the University, there were peace
parades on campus (5,000 at one time) urging "America First"
and an isolationist policy concerning the great conflict in Europe.
I was a member of the Fellowship of Reconciliation and admired
Mahatma Gandhi. Also a Modern European History course
revealed an exposé of the fraudulent propaganda for World War I
and the revelation of the "White Papers" a lot like the later
"Pentagon Papers." I was frankly unenthusiastic about war and
had strong pacifist leanings. Of course, this was long before the
horrendous pictures of the death camps were taken when Allied
armies broke through and rescued those poor skeletons of human
beings. Later in life I have vacillated on this issue, but at the time
of the draft, I was listing myself as a conscientious objector. The
draft board, however, chose my pre-theological Greek Studies
and intention to enter the seminary as the category of exemption
they decided to grant. Later in life I considered being a Navy
Chaplain; maybe I could not shoot someone in the head, but I
could comfort those who must. That did not materialize because I
have amblyopia in one eye, which did not meet the standard of
physical fitness.

So it was off to the Norwegian Lutheran Theological
Seminary in Saint Paul in the summer of 1944.

CHAPTER VII

TWO KINDS OF THEOLOGY

Theology comes in many styles much like many human personalities. After all, it is personalities that create theologies. Lately, psychosomaticists have described two types of personality: Type A (compulsive, rigid, and tense) and Type B (relaxed, laid back, and less hurried). I experienced both types of theology in the next twenty-four months.

Type A. *Den gamle Synode*
(The Old Norwegian Synod)

In retrospect I can only compare going from the University of Minnesota to the Norwegian Seminary with my experience in Finland, leaving the ultra hot and steaming sauna and jumping into the 55 degree Baltic Sea. It almost took my breath away. For one thing, the tempo was increased because of the war, around the clock and around the calendar. The incoming class started right after college commencements in June. When medical schools put the pressure on, there were some deleterious results from lack of vacation time. The University of Michigan Medical School lost several students to tuberculosis since their resistance was down. It was a pressure cooker.

My good brother, Joe, just graduating, tried to help me make the transition and suggested various of his study and note-taking methods. It was true, theological education was going to be quite different. Jack Preus had been his classmate, and therein lies a tale. He was the epitome of orthodoxy and what the Germans call *"die reine Lehre,"* in Jack's case, the 120 percent "pure teaching." He found the strict Norwegian Synod not strict enough so transferred to a splinter sect, "The Little Norwegian Synod." Here too there was loose thinking, so he switched to the severely austere Missouri Synod, which, as everyone knows, is *"ganz bestimmt"* (entirely definite). When he became President and shepherd of that flock, he found the Concordia Seminary in Saint Louis too loose and fired half of the faculty. If your microscope is powerful enough, it is amazing how many germs, microbes, and viruses you can find in anything.

Jack's next of kin, Bob, was my classmate. I have no way of verifying this, but I had the impression that when he entered the dining room, he took a glance under the table to see if there might be a heretic around. It was an awesome thing how many seminarians needed to be on their guard not only concerning their own "thought, word, and deed," but that of others as well.

When President Gullixson and his wife entertained our class at Christmas open house in their campus home, it was a solemn event indeed. His countenance resembled that of Abraham Lincoln, dour, serious, and appearing to be generally unhappy. It was some years later that I found out the poor man had experienced a life-shattering event. He had backed over his child in his driveway and the child had died. I was sorry I had been so critical of the man, and had vowed to be more accepting of others. After all, hadn't I learned about grace at the Speech Clinic? Many stigmas are borne in silence for years, and many poor souls are never really healed. We should "judge not, that we be not judged," said our teacher, Jesus.

Tension, stress, and stiffness were reflected in the faculty. There was a time during that school year that only one professor was allowed to take on extra speaking or preaching assignments because the others were under doctor's orders to cut back and slow down. They were reported to be suffering from ulcers, hypertension, and other maladies. One professor, while lecturing about "the peace that passeth understanding," was straining at the bit so hard that blood vessels stuck out in his neck and throbbed like they had too much blood in them. It was a caution.

The only healthy one was Professor Gustav Marius Bruce, who entered into no theological debate whatsoever. He taught New Testament using the Greek with meticulous precision. We went through about a chapter-and-a-half of the Gospel of John in one semester. Chapter 1, verse 1 goes like this:

ΚΑΤΑ ΙΩΑΝΝΗΝ

Ἐν ἀρχῇ ἦν ὁ λόγος, καὶ ὁ λόγος ἦν πρὸς τὸν θεόν, καὶ θεὸς ἦν ὁ λόγος.

ACCORDING TO JOHN

In the beginning was the Word, and the
Word was with God, and the Word was God.

After the lecture, he would make a pencil mark where he ended, and the next time he would erase his mark and continue for another hour. He had followed these notes faithfully for years. Not much changes in Greek. Either the verb is in the second aorist or it is not. At the end of the class period, he crossed the street and had a cup of coffee with his wife. Right after his last lecture of the week, he and his wife got into their car and headed for South Dakota to check on their farm and to look out upon the world, not the whole world (cosmos) and certainly not the worldly world, but world as in geography, their land, their own fertile piece of the world in eastern South Dakota. That's where they found the "peace that passeth understanding." He was healthy as a horse though a very old man.

I was perplexed to say the least. Those who got all embroiled in theological debate and controversy got sick over it; and Bruce, who did not get involved, was fit as a fiddle. I hoped Bryngelson would not find out about this. Where was the "Balm of Gilead," and a "… river, the streams whereof shall make glad the city of God?" What of the joy of Miriam at the water's edge? "Miriam … took a timbrel in her hand; and all the women went out after her with timbrels and with dances."

Oh, oh, the very mention of dances reminds me of the time I got into trouble and Dr. Gullixson called me into his office. To earn my way I was fortunate to get a half-time job as Secretary of the YMCA on the Ag Campus just six blocks east of the Seminary. I received $90 a month and bought myself a jacket. Sixty foreign graduate students came out to our discussion group and things were going swimmingly. I was honored to be asked to lead some community singing at the Forestry School's Paul Bunyan Dance during the intermission. I was in my element and looked upon the opportunity as a testimony to my success and popularity. Dr. Gullixson did not see it that way. When he had ascertained that I had not actually danced myself, he cautioned me thus: "By your very presence there it could be construed that you were approving of dancing. We must be careful not to lead others into temptation." There was a rumor that the Dean of Women at one of our church colleges cautioned against stand-up sex since it could lead to dancing. I doubt if this was literally true, maybe a misunderstanding. Satan lurked behind every corsage, and it was no joke; I knew that much. I did not even try to justify myself by explaining that by leading them in community singing I was at least distracting them from their baser thoughts for a time. Maybe the Forestry School would modify their program by having me lead singing most of the evening with only a short intermission for dancing.

Several of us from state universities came under increasing suspicion for liberalism in both life and learning. Meanwhile party spirit and factionalism increased so that both students and faculty took sides on various issues. This grew as smaller and smaller issues became important. It was at this time that I learned that no group is so small that it should not divide into two groups: high church vs. low church, conservative vs. liberal, pietist vs. cold fish, etc.

Another trend I saw emerging from the fragmentation and proliferation of definitions, explanations and theological theories. First there is the Bible, sufficient guide for faith and life. This is synthesized in the Apostles' or Nicene Creed, which in turn is explained, elaborated upon and interpreted. A confessional statement, such as the Augsburg Confession, further interprets, defines and elucidates the finer points. Finally, at the Norwegian Seminary, there arose a heated controversy over whether one should adopt the First Form or the Second Form of the "Minneapolis Thesis." A lot of this left me quite cold because I remembered how I had given up Speech Pathology for this greater opportunity of helping people with the stresses of life, not seeking ways of adding to their burdens.

There were about eight of us in my class that came under the suspicion of not fitting into the mold acceptable to the faculty. Yet the faculty did not want to dismiss a few of us as bad apples since that would look discriminatory. The faculty determined upon a more objective and systematic way of screening out those who would not be suitable for the ministry due to their attitude, beliefs or behavior. It is true some of us clowned around to relieve the tension, things that could well have seemed sacrilegious or, at best, disrespectful. They decided to interview the entire student body, all 150 of us, during the hottest July and August in many a year. There was no air conditioning. The already over-stressed faculty spent every afternoon after classes in a stuffy room interrogating us one by one, some for a whole hour, when they should have been out on the golf course. I can't even remember if Professor Bruce was able to work it into his schedule.

To make a long story short, toward the end of my interview, I was sure I saw the handwriting on the wall; and it said, "Transfer to Northwestern Lutheran Theological Seminary in Minneapolis. Move to Type B."

Type B. A Breath of Fresh Air

In mid-August I appeared before the small faculty of Northwestern Lutheran Theological Seminary, housed in several of the old Pillsbury mansions across from the Art Institute. The main building was the palatial mansion of John S. Pillsbury. The floor I crossed was made of solid teakwood planks eight inches wide. The President's office had an antique fireplace that was mistakenly shipped to Minneapolis instead of to J.P. Morgan's mansion in New York City, which got the Pillsbury one. What's a fireplace more or less among millionaires? The woodwork on the walls of President Roth's office was imported from England, stripped from some bankrupt Duke's castle and hand-rubbed with beeswax. The faculty looked relaxed, one smoking a pipe and one a cigar. I shook hands all around, and was offered a seat across the room from the President, who sat behind a carved desk.

The admissions interview went off more like a cozy kaffee klatsch than serious business. They had read my documents alright, but fortunately they were not turned off by the letter from President Gullixson, who wrote, "I pray that Mr. Belgum will develop a greater respect for the Word." President Roth said, "That's good enough for us; welcome to Northwestern.

We're glad to have you among us." I was later to learn that this free-wheeling seminary was accustomed to receiving students dropped, expelled or fleeing from the conservative crowd.

I had seen P.H. Roth, whose field was Church History, as one of the more exciting speakers at the L.S.A. at the University. His lecture about the life and work of Martin Luther was as intimate as a chat about a neighbor down the street and was packed with insightful and little-known information. His sense of humor was bubbly and spontaneous as jolly Santa Claus' and his frame also resembled that other saint; his belly bounced with laughter like a bowl full of Jello. His optimistic spirit was contagious.

The first day of the fall term was "Skip Day." The entire student body and all the faculty skipped out to Dean Dressler's cottage on Lake Minnetonka. Mrs. Smith, the cook, provided the ham sandwiches and potato salad; and from somewhere there appeared a keg of beer (Yes, there were quite a few Germans among them.). When I walked down to the lake after lunch, there was President Roth, standing by the shore and near a rowboat tied up to a dock. He asked me, "Do you want to go for a boat ride? I can ride if you can row." And we were off for a friendly chat on the water. The handwriting on the wall was so prophetic; this was the right place for me.

Speaking of the cook, Mrs. Smith, her presence was felt in the very air. During mid-morning Chapel Service, the aroma of her freshly baked donuts or cinnamon rolls wafted down the hall from her kitchen to our worship, and we knew we would soon be truly blessed during coffee break. The chapel period itself was a contrast with my former seminary where students used their practice sermons as polemical opportunities to champion one side or another of an argument. Attendance there was sparse and reluctant. Here attendance was almost unanimous and taken for granted about like breakfast and lunch. The students were supportive and appreciative of each other. I loved it.

Professor Hayes' New Testament course made use of *The Moffat New Testament Commentary* (1928), which made use of modern textual and historical criticism and research. There was no fear that scholarly research would detract from the value of the Word of God. The work of this Oxford trained commentator and exegete was very suspect in conservative circles, but at Northwestern it was taken for granted as helpful insight. These folks were well into the twentieth century. The Gospels came alive for me as dynamic and relevant story and realistic experience. The Bible was not mechanical but functional, as relevant beside the Sea of Galilee as on the shore of Lake Minnetonka. Everything was coming together for me, and I was glad.

Financially, the way was eased generously. Not only was there no tuition; at the end of my admissions interview, President Roth said, "Oh, by the way, we give everyone a hundred dollar scholarship." There was only the reasonable Boarding Club fee and books. Then, to top it off, someone said Pastor John Simmons at Saint Mark, on the North Side, was looking for a student to help out. I went out there to see the church next Sunday. While standing around afterwards chatting with folks, I had two invitations to dinner, no doubt a friendly place. They did not know I was a seminarian. When John was done shaking hands, I introduced myself, and he hired me on the spot. There I worked throughout my senior year.

John Simmons was a continuation of the fresh air program. He was a bundle of energy and raucous humor, teasing people including me. In just a few years he had built up the congregation from 300 to 800 and the budget had risen dramatically. He was deeply involved in community affairs and constantly invited to speak at this and that group meeting. Sometimes there would be breakfast, lunch and dinner speeches all in the same day. He was influential and key in settling the great Bell Telephone strike. To oust a crooked alderman on the North Side, he gathered a group of tough ex-Marines to guard the voting places and the ballot boxes. Then they rode more or less shotgun with the ballot boxes down to the Court House. Since it was the first time the ballots had been counted, the crooked alderman did not have a chance. John figured if the Marines fought for democracy elsewhere, they could also stick up for it on the North side. PUT THE GOSPEL TO WORK, ACTION, NOW! It was a circus and a great way to start out in the ministry. I was much indebted to him for such a positive beginning.

John and I hit it off so well that he persuaded the congregation to call me as their first Assistant Pastor upon my graduation. In due course I received an official Letter of Call from Saint Mark indicating that I "had been issued a call by unanimous decision of the congregation." I was flabbergasted; imagine me, an ordinary, run-of-the-mill seminarian of humble birth receiving <u>unanimous</u> endorsement. I shared the letter with John waving it before him with smile from ear to ear. He chuckled and oriented me to the real world of parliamentary procedure. "Do you want me to tell you what the vote was that they make it unanimous, Dave?" I got the point, but it was still O.K.

The family got together for my graduation and ordination. The Faculty graciously invited my father to preach the Baccalaureate sermon. We went to a cabin in Northern Minnesota just like in the good old days. All systems were go and I was ready to begin my career as Pastor Belgum.

John Simmons was wholehearted and full of the best intentions. The first week he said, "Dave, we gotta get our exercise and take a day off a week. Tomorrow, we go bowling." The next week we did some other recreation, and that was the end of that as busy scheduling of speaking and meetings filled his date book. He was most supportive of me. He said, "We'll divide up the preaching, but the people don't need to know who will preach when. They should come to worship, learn, and serve regardless of who's in the pulpit." I could not have had a better mentor nor gotten a better start.

I had to get used to fulfilling a role. For example, one elderly lady was obviously using me to fulfill the role of a nice son she never had. Her own son was a scoundrel who cared for her not at all. As I called on her from time to time as a pastoral care giver, I had not realized how subjective the relationship had become for her. I assumed I was simply Herr Pastor doing my ministerial rounds as well as I could. Then she gave me a new expensive watch as a gift. Perplexed and bothered, I showed it to John and wondered what in the world to do--Could she afford it? And I was only doing my pastoral duty and was paid by the church. Was this ethical?? John simply assured me that evidently <u>she needed</u> to do something <u>nice</u> for her "son." I should not reject her. I saw I'd have much to learn.

How and where could I learn more about pastoral care and counseling? I felt my skills and insights were woefully lacking. There were four centers in the United States at that time that had graduate programs in this field: Southern California University, the University of Chicago, Union Seminary in New York City, and Boston University. The latter seemed to suit me best for my purpose. Besides, there was a little Danish Lutheran Church only a couple miles from the school which was vacant and needed a so-called part-time interim during their vacancy, which in my case lasted five years until I received my doctorate in June of 1952. So it was off to Boston.

CHAPTER VIII

CAN A LITTLE 4-H CLUB MEMBER
BECOME A BOSTONIAN?

My contact or liaison with the church in Boston was Bill Larsen, a Dane who had served them just prior to entering the Marine Chaplaincy. He had also studied in Boston. I had known him as a successor to Carl Lund-Quist as campus pastor at the University of Minnesota during my seminary days. Currently, he was serving in the same role at Ohio State University in Columbus. I saddled up my 1940 V-8 Ford, put my shirts, underwear and socks in a suitcase and took off. I figured a side trip to see Bill would be a good way to get some low-down on my new charge and learn where those Danish Lutherans were coming from.

Bill and Inga welcomed me warmly and shared many things. He had a sense of humor and a winning smile. He explained how the *Indre Mission* (Inner Mission type) were from the pietist branch of the church of Denmark. "But they will take a little wine on a festive occasion. And when the Pastor calls, that's a festive occasion." I replied, "So they're a little inconsistent; I can handle it." He assured me they were warm and sincere people, but of course stoical like other Scandinavians. Being a Norwegian I should fit in just fine.

When I had my first visit to see whether they would officially call me to the post, I had a very interesting orientation to Boston. I was driven, from where they had put me up for the night, along a lovely parkway, Jamaica Way, by a languid pond and some flower gardens; and then a couple quick turns and we were at Bethany, a most attractive though small church set off by a low stone wall and an ornamental cast iron fence. It was only

87

after I got settled that I saw how far out of the way they had to
escort me to avoid the grimmer aspects of the slums of Roxbury.
Oh, it would be a challenge alright; but I was game for anything.
Here I was the total staff of a church of a hundred members. Is a
hundred to one good odds? I was on my own in a city populated
mostly by Irish Catholics. The four denominational headquarters
there were Unitarian-Universalist, Christian Science,
Congregationalist and Swedenborgian. It would be quite different
from Pope County and even Lutheran Minneapolis.

Since I was a bachelor, the Council hit upon an excellent
plan that would kill two birds with one stone. They asked Metha
Knudsen to take me in as a boarder. She had a lovely home in
Roslindale and was about sixty-five years of age and had lost her
husband a few years ago. There was the danger that she might
move to Chicago and live with her daughter, who had married a
wealthy old bachelor in the scavenger business. Then they would
lose not only a member but their organist as well, a musician who
usually played "Shepherd Song" as a prelude. If she could feel
some moral obligation to house and feed the new minister, that
would be great. She agreed.

I was most fortunate. From my perspective it was as
though I had an eight-room house with a full-time maid. Out of
my salary of $1,600 a year, I was to pay her $35 a month.
Tuition at Boston University was $500, so you see I still had
money left for foolishness, like clothes, gas and car insurance,
which in Boston, with all its traffic circles, was horrendous, $200
a year. I knew almost nothing about money and thought a
"savings account" was something Emperor Charlemagne had for
spending money, but would certainly not be a concern for a
member of the proletariat like my humble self. Nor did I have
any life insurance. As a bachelor, I figured as long as I had
enough paid into my old car to cover the cost of a pine box for

my final rooming place, I was being totally responsible. I had not learned how to be a financial wizard from my Papa.

<u>Danks Evangeliske Lutherske Kirke</u>
<u>i Boston og Omeng</u>
Danish Evangelical Lutheran Church
in Boston and Vicinity

The artistic interior--work of
the faithful members

The gracefully proportioned church had been built by early members since most of the immigrants came from the trades-- carpentry, bricklaying, painting and others. Isiduro Rasmussen was also an interior decorator, who could decorate a bank to look like an Egyptian temple or a Renaissance town hall. The altar painting, the grapevine beginning at the altar and going down both sides of the church, symbolizing "I am the vine, ye are the branches," the plaster pillars painted to look like marble and the inscription above the arch were all painted by members. The inscription read:

> *Herren er I sit hellige Temple*
> *Stille for hans Ansicht al Jorden.*
>
> The Lord is in His holy Temple
> Let all the world be still before His face.

The altar, communion rail, pulpit, baptismal font and all the pews were hand shaped by skilled cabinetmakers. What pride they took in their work. You knew you were in a church; and I felt like a pastor in the pulpit and before the altar.

Seventy-eight percent of the members had Danish surnames, whereas most of the remainder were camouflaged by intermarriage with "foreigners" or a stray Yankee or two. Although they had settled in Roxbury, by the time I arrived, the members had scattered to seventeen suburbs and towns, the furthest distance being forty miles. Within the first six months I was able to call on all of them and get acquainted, or so I thought. One lady wasn't so sure I knew her after four years. On a bright and cheerful Sunday morning, I was in high spirits shaking hands at the front door after service. Thinking I knew her well by now, I chanced the following greeting: "Good morning <u>Marie</u>!" She responded briskly, "<u>It IS Mrs. Fischer</u>!"

I was also addressed with considerable formality and status. It was at least <u>Pastor</u> Belgum, but, as often as not, it was simply "Good morning Pastor," or "Oh, Pastor, I wanted to ask you a question." Sometimes I felt I was not a <u>person</u> so much as a function or a condition, "pastorhood" or "condition of pastor" or "the function of pastoring." Actually, I felt very much at home with this, because in my studies of Psychology of Religion, this very dynamic interested me enough to write my Ph.D. dissertation on *The Role of the Chaplain in the Care of the Patient,* and it became the subject (revised for public consumption) of my first book, published by Westminster Press. What constitutes a <u>role</u> and how do reciprocal roles interact, like between shopkeeper and customer, physician and patient, husband and wife, parent and child, etc.? I studied how chaplains and others perceived the <u>role</u> of chaplain. I took my parishioners' message as saying, "We want to use you in the role of pastor." And, of course, that is exactly what I had signed up for.

It took this midwesterner awhile to get used to the New England ethos. Mrs. Knudsen's neighbor was an old-line jeweler who drove a 1926 Essex with wooden spoke wheels. He brought his diamonds home with him in papers in a Boston Bag rather than leave them in the store where they might be stolen. I had lived next to him for a year, but we had not spoken. Bostonians do not rush into relationships. This July afternoon as I came home from work, he was alone on the verandah because his sister had left for Cape Cod early. He hailed me thus: "Would the Rector join me on the verandah for a Coke and a cigarette?" Needless to say, I quickly grabbed the chance not knowing when another invitation might come along. It did come next year. He and his sister invited Metha and me for a Saturday night supper of Boston Baked Beans and Brown Bread, an established institution. The bowl of beans was about eight inches from my plate, but he rang the bell for their maid, Katherine, for assistance. She did not respond, so he went out to the kitchen and asked her, "Katherine, would you please come and pass the Rector the beans." And she did. And I took some. And I said, "Thank you." And I ate them. And we went home.

Having a parish served as a wonderful laboratory for my studies in Psychology of Religion, Pastoral Care and Counseling, Religion and Mental Health, and similar courses at Boston University. My fellow graduate students also had small parishes for their self-support. A previous janitor at Bethany had gotten into the Communion wine, and evidently a good deal of other wine too. The poor man caused himself some brain damage and finally ended up as a hopeless case at Boston State Hospital. He was so out of it that his wife had to sew name tags on his clothes and shoes and socks. He hardly knew her after fifty years of marriage. Norwegian is enough like Danish, so I began the Lord's Prayer thinking it might hook a connection in the deeper recesses of his memory.

> *Fader vor, du some er in himlene!*
> *Helliget vorde dit navn!*
> *Komme dit rike!* (sic: the ritual book used the !)

His eyes began to focus on me and my clerical collar, and gradually he began to share with me his early memories of church life in Denmark. As a boy he had sung in a quartet for funerals, and many other things. Nothing could have made me more receptive to Carl Gustav Jung's research and discussion of the Unconscious and the power of Symbols.

Another lady caught me off guard. In her early eighties she lived in a cold-water flat typical of a worn-out slum. Coal gas oozed into the hallway and stairwells and under the flimsy doors to the one-room compartments. She had reason to feel grumpy because one of the deacons had suggested she put the life savings she had earned by housework into Longwood Towers, an elegant apartment complex built just before the crash of 1929. She lost everything and subsisted now on Old Age Assistance. She was as frail and flimsy as a wraith, especially her hands, which had veins like strands of purple knitting yarn under her translucent skin. Yet, she remained a deeply devout person and looked forward to the first Sunday of the month when I would bring Communion immediately after we had celebrated it at church only two blocks away.

On this particular noon, I was feeling especially warmly pastoral, the young pastor postponing his Sunday dinner as he served this poor old woman. It was a sincere dedication and it felt right. She laid out a cloth on a small table near her over-stuffed chair with a lighted candle in place, like a home altar. I first had a brief visit while I was setting up my materials, the Bread and the Wine, for a private service. I took out my pocket-sized *Occasional Services Book,* which also had funerals and wedding liturgies, and reverently continued to the end with the final blessing. As I turned to put away the vessels, I could be excused for my warm spiritual glow and expectation of the thanks and gratitude she would express to me for my ministry. When I turned around to shake her hand, she said in a loud voice, "I haven't had a bowel movement in three days." As I walked down the street I laughed to myself and kicked myself in the behind for being so sure I knew what to expect in any situation. She died shortly after that, which is what she earnestly wanted. Her funeral was one of the ten I had that year.

Next to the church was a run-down, formerly elegant duplex, which had been converted into four five-room apartments. A fairly irresponsible G.I. had bought it but could not hold onto it. It had citations against it for code violation for fire, plumbing and electricity--totally unsafe. The substructure was as solid as when it was built one hundred and twenty-five years earlier. It was getting near Christmas and I offered the owner to take over his loan and give him $50 in cash. He accepted; I was a landlord. Metha Knudsen went to live with her daughter in Chicago, and I was on my own. I lived in one upper apartment and took in a Latvian refugee family of mother, father and an eight-year-old girl. The rents, including my own $35 allowance, covered the remaining mortgage payments including the $800 home improvement loan, which the bank was glad to extend so we could get all the citations removed and bring it into line with all the city codes. When I sold it later, I cleared enough to buy a new Plymouth four-door sedan. I was getting a little smarter in the financial arena.

The president of the congregation, Martin Petersen, was a gem, as were so many of the solid citizens who had made it up from nothing as immigrants. One Sunday he and his wife invited me home for dinner after church. On the way we picked up a couple sizable lobsters and I saw them boiled alive. The Petersens lived out by the shore in Lynn, north of Boston. In the afternoon he took me sailing on Nahant Bay. What a life! During the visit I managed to transact several important matters of church business, which passed at the next council meeting. Just because it was work doesn't mean it couldn't be enjoyable.

The church, and my new domicile, were only a mile from the ocean, and a streetcar went directly to the "L" Street Bathhouse. Sometimes I took the "Dirty Aces" swimming, a gang so disruptive they were expelled from the Norfolk Settlement House. There were times when I would board and pay my fare and look around to find none of my boys in sight. They were hanging on the back rather than wasting money on a fare. During the opening session of Vacation Bible School, after I had moved to Roxbury, all seven of these villains clomped down the center aisle with their leader carrying a railroad tie. (The publicity stated that each pupil should bring enough wood to make a cross during crafts time.) The leader said cockily, "Is this big enough for you?" I complimented him by announcing to the entire group assembled that this pupil had clearly brought the largest piece of wood. Congratulations! Now he was stuck trying to make a cross out of it. We got along fine.

Boston was such a rich cultural experience. It was like being in another country, history galore. I discovered that the Boston Tea Party site is now two blocks inland since the harbor has been filled in so much. Old Ironsides, ship of the Revolutionary War vintage, lay in a nearby harbor. I explored Bunker Hill, the Old North Church of Paul Revere fame, Beacon Hill and much more. One browse I especially relished was my bi-weekly visit to Ye Olde Union Oyster House. There I would join a motley range of persons, practically all men, around a semi-circular soapstone counter, all waiting for our half dozen on the half shell. There was a tart sauce for dipping and the little hexagon crackers. As the ad says, "It doesn't get any better than this." Up on Louisberg Square some elderly dowagers objected to having the old brick sidewalk replaced with modern concrete. They brought out their chairs and sat themselves down. The street department decided not to haul the bricks and the ladies away in dump trucks, and the historic sidewalk remained. One of the tenants in my apartment house was a bribe collector for Mayor Curley and a dispenser of patronage. You recall that Curley was re-elected Mayor when he was serving time in Norfolk State Prison. I knew either he or one of his aides would show up at a Catholic wake and present a wreath for the casket in the living room. Then a ten dollar bill would be handed soulfully to the poor widow with a heartfelt condolence for all to see. He was tithing, giving back a tenth of what he had stolen from the city the previous hour.

One Christmas Eve I visited the top and bottom of society within two hours. I visited the very sick wife of our janitor, whose house was assessed for tax purposes as worth $600. There I had a cup of coffee from an old cracked cup, and we had good fellowship. Later I was privileged to drink Christmas Egg Nog from a crystal cup on Beacon Hill in the home of the interior decorator of Filene's Department Store. The elegant chandeliers in the dining room and living room glistened as we looked out the full-length French windows overlooking the red-robed boys' choir from the Episcopal Cathedral caroling and ringing their bells on Beacon Street below. Ironically, I was appropriately dressed at both sites because my black suit and clerical collar was the only dress-up outfit I owned.

But we must get back to the main reason I had come to Boston--to study and improve myself professionally and personally. Nothing showed me more clearly how much more I needed to learn than my pastoral experience at Saint Mark and at Bethany.

The dates of my study in Boston were 1947 to 1952. How did that time frame stand in relation to the growing interest in Psychology of Religion and Pastoral Care and Counseling as fields of study?

William James, who wrote the classic *Varieties of Religious Experience* in 1902, taught at Harvard, just across the Charles River from Boston. Freud and Jung arrived from Europe as guest lecturers at Clark University just forty miles west of Boston in 1908. Freud's attempt to apply psychoanalytic principles to religion came out in his *Moses and Monotheism* in 1939 just eight years before I arrived in Boston. Jung's stimulating and ironic

Modern Man In Search of A Soul was a rapprochement between psychiatry and religion published in 1933. Gordon W. Allport, another Harvard professor, an Episcopal layman, whose textbook I had used at Minnesota, wrote an excellent, short treatment of *The Individual and His Religion* during my stay in Boston, 1950. The field was being worked by many planters and cultivators. I wanted to harvest some of these insights.

World War II brought on a rash of interest in counseling, especially anything that would be helpful for military personnel recovering from battle fatigue and other consequences of service such as readjustment to civilian life, vocational guidance, etc. Military chaplains had demonstrated their worth.

Richard Cabot, eminent Harvard Medical School professor and staff member at Massachusetts General Hospital, saw an analogy between the need for medical students to have hands-on clinical experience and the theological student's need for putting theory into practice. In a 1925 issue of *The Survey,* Cabot published "A Plea for a Clinical Year in the Course of Theological Study." Together with Chaplain Russell Dicks of Massachusetts General Hospital, he authored a book entitled *The Art of Ministering to the Sick* (1936). Anton Boisen returned in 1925 to the Worcester State Hospital, where he had himself been a patient, to begin a chaplaincy program and admit four theological students to study "the human document," to explore the relation of religion to mental illness both diagnostically and therapeutically.

The time and the place were full of ferment concerning religion and personality development, religion and mental health and religion and psychosomatic dynamics.

Paul E. Johnson was the catalytic agent who created a graduate program by arranging laboratory experience in the many institutions of the Boston area: Massachusetts General

Hospital, Boston Psychopathic Hospital, Boston City Hospital, Boston Dispensary and Judge Baker Guidance Center. These served as clinical experience for courses in counseling and group dynamics as well as possible grist for the Ph.D. dissertation mill. He was a creative coordinator. I did not know what I would do with all this experience and education, but I was relishing every minute of it. I had almost become a Bostonian to boot.

CHAPTER IX

REAL ROMANCE AT LAST

The most wonderful experience in Boston was romantic, neither academic nor ecclesiastical. It came about in a strange way as I understand true romance often does. Oh, I had been trying to generate romance for many years; after all, I was an aging gentleman of twenty-eight years of bachelorhood. And I didn't like it. Then this Yankee couple who had come to Boston from Portland, Maine, via the University of Michigan, showed up at Bethany Church. One Ash Wednesday evening they walked through eighteen inches of snow for a mile-and-a-half to attend the Vesper Service. It's a wonder they came back because one of my trusty Danes was shocked when introduced to them: "Stevens, that's not Danish; is it?" Then the boy friend's turn: "Watson, that's not Danish either, is it?" Like who left the back door open?

Patricia Stevens had become a Lutheran and now worked as a medical technologist in Boston. Her intended was finishing up a degree at Tufts University. They were making two transitions in life: Pat and Les were getting married, and Les was seeking instruction to join the Lutheran Church. They settled on Bethany, not that there were that many Lutheran churches in Boston to choose from.

After a few sessions of premarital counseling together with some instruction for Les in Lutheranism, Pat made an off-hand remark, "I know a nice girl for you, Pastor Belgum." Oh, good, I'd follow up on any lead, and took out my date book to record her name and phone number. "She's a sorority sister of mine and goes to school at the University of Michigan." I quickly put my prospect book away since Ann Arbor was beyond commuting distance, about an even thousand miles. "Thanks, but if you come across anyone locally, let me know." Not to be put off, she informed me, as the wedding date approached, "I don't care; you're going to meet her because she is in the wedding party." Now what?

I had received permission to perform the marriage from the Secretary of State in Maine and was all set to go. But no, Bill Larsen, who was studying at Harvard that summer, assured me I had to have an extra suit for the Rehearsal Dinner. He knew I owned only my black clerical suit with black socks and shoes to match. He lent me his brown suit, which matched my brown eyes to a "T." Having no car to my name, I stepped off the train in the Portland Railroad Station to be greeted by Les and Pat and this unusual gal, who seemed to have no legs. She was wearing a low waisted dress, which I guess was the style--how should I know? It was all very confusing to my simple mind.

I had not performed many weddings and was somewhat overwhelmed by the church organist, who complained about my rapid pace at rehearsal. She expostulated, "When will I have time to pull my pistons?" We got through it. The whole wedding party were adults and knew how to walk already, so the rehearsal was fairly brief. Then on to the EVENT, the Rehearsal Dinner, and what an occasion. The bride's father was an affluent physician and put on a fine dinner and party. Ladies in black outfits with little black and white headpieces went about filling and refilling champagne glasses. Every time I turned around my glass was full again. It reminded me of the prophet Elijah who blessed the poor widow so soundly that the "jar of meal was not spent, neither did the cruse of oil fail." But there was no widow here, and I did not resemble Elijah. I was learning by the minute, almost in time, how to act in very polite society. Meanwhile, I found myself sitting beside Kathie Geigenmueller on the steps in the hallway. My, she was a good-looking gal and so pleasant;

what a pity that Ann Arbor was light years away. The wedding went off smoothly enough followed by a grand reception at the Golf and Country Club out by the ocean. What do you know; once again Kathie and I were together strolling on the lawn gazing over the surf and occasionally at each other. She was great, tall and slender in her bridesmaid outfit. She had dark, long hair and absolutely friendly eyes. She was a picture I would not forget as I left with a parishioner couple to ride back to Boston Saturday night so I could conduct the service in Bethany in the morning.

As I walked down the aisle at Bethany, everything seemed to be well under control. The ladies were wearing their multi-colored garments--mostly navy blue, dark gray and several shades of black depending on the fabric. Their hats were entirely appropriate for *det Dansk Evangelisk Kirke i Boston og Omeng*. When I came out from the sacristy in my regalia, I paused before the altar with due reverence. When I turned around to face the congregation, there were, in the fifth pew, two of the most enormous white straw hats one could imagine. They looked especially large since the wearers were bowing in meditation (or to avoid laughing). When they raised their faces, I saw under one of the hats KATHIE GEIGENMUELLER. Now, it is not easy, under normal circumstances, to remain totally dedicated to Kingdom work; but this really took me aback. Surely you do not expect me to remember what I preached about or whether I replaced the Invocation with the Benediction. After a friendly handshake at the door, I took off for a Sunday School Picnic and they caught their continuing flight to White Sulfur Springs for a Chi Omega convention. How far is it to Ann Arbor again?

That summer I was enrolled in a Group Dynamics and Mental Health course at Boston Psychopathic Hospital. It was team-taught by the Superintendent of the hospital and the

Chaplain, who was also a graduate student at Boston University in my same program. One morning Bob Leslie, the Chaplain, announced that the Institute of Pastoral Care Program of Clinical Pastoral Education at the University of Michigan Hospital needed an assistant. It was an emergency as the one engaged was suddenly unavailable. I told Bill Larsen how sorry I was that the program was six weeks and I had only a month's vacation. He knew about Kathie. He scolded me thus: "Get out there, you fool; I'll cover for you at Bethany" (remember he'd been their pastor some years previously). So he sent me off in his brown suit, and I really couldn't believe it. And Les and Pat laughed all the way home.

We got along great in those six weeks, and I knew my search was totally over. But what about Kathie? She seemed to enjoy my company. We played tennis and each weekend went to her folks' cottage on the shore of Lake Erie for swimming, barbecuing and generally finding out what it was like to live in Heaven. The six weeks were up too soon.

As the fall wore on, Kathie's enthusiasm faded for reasons I did not understand. Only some years later she shared the fact that what was left of my stuttering was not all that attractive. Just because I, a distinguished graduate of the Speech Clinic, was blasé about stuttering did not mean everyone was; all of which reminds of the famous case of the judge with lack of bladder control, especially after sitting on the stained Bench for long periods. His family physician referred him to a urologist; but instead of getting off at the fifth floor and turning left to room 506, he had disembarked at the third floor and entered 306, a psychiatrist's office. After six months, His Honor encountered his family physician on the street and was asked how things were going. The judge responded, "Oh, I still do that, but it doesn't bother me anymore." Well, evidently it still bothered Kathie more than I realized. Also, it had been her intention to marry a "jock," and I was not a star athlete. Oh, we had many good tennis games, some of which I won; but I was not a gung ho competitor. Most sports to me were just games.

I practically invited myself to her home for a visit over Christmas. I would leave Boston two minutes after my Christmas Service and head West like Brigham Young looking for the Promised Land. Meanwhile, Kathie informed me that it would be best if I not come since she had seriously injured her knee in a basketball game and it was in a long cast. In my case the motto worth repeating was "You don't hear what you don't want to hear." I thought, "The poor girl. If there ever were a person who needed pastoral care it was surely Kathie Geigenmueller." I drove even faster into the sunset. Things went gradually downhill after that.

After a spring, summer and fall of dormancy, the embers somehow seemed to glow again, because, while I was mailing her a Christmas present record of E. Power Biggs playing Bach on the pipe organ, Kathie was mailing me a pair of hand-knit Argyle socks. I could not have been happier. Now, for the third summer I assisted Chaplain Ballinger at University of Michigan Hospital, this time again a welcome visitor at the Geigenmueller cottage on Lake Erie. I went through the proper formalities and Herr Geigenmueller, impressive leader of the family, gave his consent quite willingly, and Mrs. Geigenmueller gladly seconded the motion. By this time I had finished my Ph.D. program at Boston University and earned enough points to become a fully certified Chaplain Supervisor of a Clinical Pastoral Education Program if such an opportunity opened up.

How in the world did
David complete his
dissertation with·
that photo on his dresser?

Could the Pastor be
violating a relative's
admonition "not to
have too much fun?"
Yes, in Michigan.

All I needed now was a job. I sent out my resume to twenty-nine sites which might be interested in a Professor of Religion, a Chaplain Supervisor or a Parish Pastor. I was especially eager to get settled because Kathie and I had agreed that we would wait to get married until I had a position. We were still of the old school.

The President of the Central Pennsylvania Synod replied that, yes, indeed, they had thirty parishes vacant; but since I now had a Ph.D. I would no doubt be unable to speak on the level of common parishioners. I drew a blank on seven other synods. I should have used Scope or maybe even Listerine. Twelve months after my letter-writing barrage, I received a letter from the Superintendent of the State Hospital at Helena, Montana, saying they were hoping to develop a program in the future. "Hey, man, I want to get married yesterday!"

I did receive one positive response from Wittenberg College, Springfield, Ohio. It turned into an offer of accepting me to join their ranks as Assistant Professor of Religion. I was ecstatic. The acceptance came at Christmas to take effect the following September at the beginning of the new fall term. We set our wedding date for August 8, 1953.

Meanwhile, I kept food in my mouth by working in the Education Department of Ypsilanti State Hospital about a dozen miles south of Ann Arbor. Kathie worked as a Medical Technologist at University of Michigan Hospital. My position of Teacher/Therapist was an enriching experience since the youthful clients were a double challenge. These were kids who were both mentally ill and delinquents mostly. They were incorrigible in detention centers and failures in mental health centers. We were the end of the line--the Psychic Cesspool of Michigan Youth. Our Director, Mr. Potter, was ideally suited for this reality-testing, no foolishness, "tough love" program. Under him wonders happened; yet, for practically all of them, it was a long-term program, sometimes years. Their heads had been so messed up by their parents it was unbelievable. A thirteen-year-old was already a confirmed kleptomaniac and an established sociopath. His morals were 180° opposite from society. His father taught him how to steal car batteries from auto supply stores and rewarded him for this "good behavior." He was punished for failing to steal properly. Another young fellow from Detroit knew how to make a gun that would shoot accurately up to a hundred feet. It was made of hardened steel pipe and triggered by a rubber band cut from an auto inner tube.

In the workshop, where the student-clients created all sorts of things, I was struck by the exceedingly vulgar language. Elwood, building a birdhouse, repeatedly said, "God damn thus and so." I tried a technique I had not learned anywhere but which was motivated by my curiosity about their linguistics.

"Elwood, I notice you are praying, and that's OK. But I'm puzzled. I thought you were trying to build the birdhouse up; but I hear you praying that God will tear it down, condemn it. Which way are you really trying to go?" Here was no castigation for profanity, which he might have expected since they all knew I was a minister. I was just taking his words seriously and assumed he literally meant what he said. You see, no one had ever taken his speech seriously since he did not even count as a person where he came from.

Andy was angry in Math class (actually elementary arithmetic). He shouted, "Fuck this arithmetic book." I inquired how it was possible to have sexual intercourse with an arithmetic book; wouldn't that be awfully painful? He looked startled and puzzled. No one had ever assumed he meant what he said about anything. Where was I coming from anyway? At no time did I ever suggest they not use such language; I was just trying to understand what they were saying and what they meant by this and that word.

In a few weeks, Elwood was challenging a buddy, "Don't talk nonsense." Jake was more than an "asshole." True, he had an anus, but also arms, legs and ears. To me no word was meaningless, but I wanted to know what the meaning was for that boy at that time. He could say whatever he wanted as long as it was clear and accurate and made sense. More and more kids were saying, "Don't talk nonsense." It was a most interesting laboratory for me to continue learning about personality, especially in this early developmental stage.

And, what did this have to do with Kathie and me? We shared our mutual work experiences and got to know each other more fully as we understood each other working in the real world. Romance can be a happy flight of fancy, which is wonderful; but it should be matched by understanding each other's attitude toward work, life tasks that go on between the hugs and kisses, wonderful as they are. We had meals together in the apartment with her two roommates and the boyfriend of one of them. Both Jack and I were poor enough to be glad for a free meal now and then (increasingly more often _now_ rather than _then_). Our dating was cheap. We laugh over the first date when I offered Kathie a "lemonade drink." She had never heard of this countryfied expression, and being from the sorority crowd she had had fellows spend more than 15¢ on her in an evening.

Yes, socioeconomically Kathie and I were miles apart. While I came out of a Depression background, Kathie's father had progressed steadily upward to the point where he was now head of Monroe Steel Castings Company employing three hundred workers of many kinds. He was a very skilled and highly principled administrator whom everyone trusted. He was shrewd in business matters in a conservative and careful way that paid off

in the long run. Her family belonged to the local Country Club.
I admired and respected him. Although I had a pinko-liberal
philosophy, I would not wish him to be any other way than he
was, a rock solid Republican. If all businessmen were like Paul
Geigenmueller, the world would be a much better place. His
workers sought his advice like from a Dutch uncle, questions of
whether to buy or rent a place, whether to get married, etc. He
refused to have air conditioning in his office since his workers
were out in the foundry where it was hot winter and summer.
His men respected him, and he had a minimum of labor strife in
his plant. One Sunday when he accompanied me as I went to
supply a pulpit in Ann Arbor, he said a remarkable thing. "I
admire your ability to get up before people and speak. I could
never do that." It was a profound compliment coming from such
an accomplished and successful man. I continue to learn how
varied are the individual differences between people, the
assortment of strengths and weaknesses, hidden or revealed.
What is one person's meat is another's poison, as the saying goes.
What is one person's junk is another's antique. To one person
something is a disaster, to another the same thing is a nuisance.
What is an absolute necessity for one is a frivolous matter to
another. It was great knowing Paul Geigenmueller.

The wedding, in Monroe, was perfect: A balance between
elegance and spontaneity, reverence and fun. It was hard to
believe Kathie was coming down the aisle to join her life with
mine for the rest of our lives (which will be forty years next
summer). Pastor Heine had graciously invited my father to share
in the service. Kathie's Aunty Bert moved out of her apartment
and made it available for my folks. The hospitality was genuine
and abundant. At the reception out at the Country Club, Papa
enjoyed himself immensely. He drank freely of what he thought
was the best lemonade he had ever tasted. Actually it was

champagne, but it led to no problem. Maybe he just pretended he thought it was lemonade.

The following photo shows the matchmakers, Les and Pat, toasting us as we had toasted them. "It doesn't get any better than this." Or did it? Oh, yes it did. Our honeymoon was great. I had arranged for the Whittier Hotel on the Detroit River and had elan enough to have champagne waiting on ice. This was going to be no 4-H Club meeting. The one hitch of the evening was the fact that I was totally unable to get the cork out of the bottle and had to send for a room service person to do the honors. Everything went well after that; and that's all I'm going to say!

Next morning we journeyed on to Algonquin Provincial Park north of Toronto. The elegant lodge was across a small lake, so one had to park the car and ring for a barge to come and get you--hence no vehicles on the grounds. We had our own cabin with ample firewood for the stone fireplace, and took our meals in a gracious dining room with large picture windows overlooking Source Lake. The kitchen staff packed a box lunch when we went canoeing for the whole day, portaging from one lake to another as a detailed map directed. Swimming and sunning were delightful alternatives. One time we were sunning so much that we had to scurry behind some bushes while six canoes full of Boy Scouts skimmed by. Naturally, I thought about Adam and Eve and wondered if this experience would ever fit into a sermon--"Oh, forget it; it's your day off."

We returned to Monroe, Michigan, as Mr. and Mrs., an old married couple, ready to head south to our first home at Springfield, Ohio. I was ready to enter upon a new personal and professional life. Best of all, I had found REAL ROMANCE AT LAST.

CHAPTER X

FINDING A VOCATION IN ACADEME

How fortunate I have been professionally. Wittenberg
College was as affirming a setting to begin teaching as Saint Mark
had been to begin ministry. The college administration rightly
guessed that their novice faculty were usually not well-heeled,
and, therefore, they owned several houses divided into apartments
that such young faculty couples could rent at cost. We had a
comfortable first-floor unit and felt very fortunate in our new
home.

Kathie obtained a job in her field of medical technology at
the local hospital. At her suggestion we put all her salary in the
bank toward the day when we might be able to buy a house. We
lived quite well, though simply, on my salary of $4,300 a year.
Kathie was far more qualified to deal with money matters than I;
so I was glad to leave that sphere to her. After forty years that
still seems to have been a very wise decision on my part. Each do
what you can do best.

Other faculty and administrators were very congenial and
friendly, so we quickly felt at home. I gave Kathie a cute
German shepherd puppy, which she enjoyed taking for a
disciplined walk and sometimes a free run on campus. We were
included in parties and asked to chaperone fraternity dances. You
can see by the photo how we enjoyed ourselves. Yes, this branch
of Lutheranism was of the same spirit as Northwestern Seminary
in Minneapolis. As far as I knew there was no higher incidence
of unmarried motherhood at Wittenberg than at Fairview Hospital
School of Nursing where the fearfully repressed Norwegian
seminarians found their parsonage mates (some of whom attended
Dr. Gullixson's Christmas Party). In fact, this reminds me of the

pietist Norwegian church college girl upon whom I had a crush in
college days. She neither danced nor would she kiss me good
night on the front porch of her home in Minneapolis. She
evidently did kiss someone else, because she became totally
pregnant out of wedlock and had to marry the man who did it.

        Teaching was a whole new ball game. In many graduate
programs a person just narrows in on some dissertation topic of
unexplored specialization. One gathers data by the bushel and
compresses it into two or three hundred pages with an average of
three footnotes per page. Then one bright spring day the
university plops a doctoral hood squarely upon your shoulders,
like a prophet's mantle, and BINGO, you are qualified to teach all
kinds of stuff, whatever is needed by the department that term.
High school and elementary teachers study "pedagogical method,"
how to create and grade exams, how to use audiovisual aids, etc.
But at the college level my degree in Psychology of Religion was
sufficient credential to teach freshmen Old Testament in the fall
and New Testament in the spring, also a course in Christian

Education for future parish workers, subjects in which I had had no further study than any of five thousand other Lutheran pastors. My colleagues in the Religion Department were helpful in initiating me into the tasks and tricks of teaching.

What floored me the second year was the request from Dean Flack that I come up on the hill to the Hamma Divinity School and teach New Testament Greek. Our conversation went about like this:

"But Dean Flack," I remonstrated, "I'm not any good at Greek. To be perfectly honest, I flunked the introductory course when I took Homeric Greek at the University of Minnesota. When I retook the course, that time in Attic Greek, I passed but never got above "C" the whole year." (I was never nicknamed either "Little Caesar" nor "Little Socrates.")

"Don't worry about it," he said in his fatherly way. "You see, I'm in a bind. I usually have an M.A. candidate who does the beginning Greek course for me for his stipend; but this fall I have no one but you. I've already spoken to the Chairman of the Department of Religion, and he'll release you to me for this five-hour-a-week course."

"What will the students think when they discover I should be wearing a Greek dunce cap and sitting on a stool facing the corner?"

"Nonsense," he replied with his best salesmanship smile. "You just take the introductory textbook by Huddleston, one lesson at a session. Drill them hard on the declensions, conjugations and, of course, the vocabulary at the end of the lesson. You remember the alphabet, don't you?" he twitted. "It's on page 5." He was having as much fun with me as any cat ever had with a mouse. "Then, if they ask anything you don't know, tell them you'll get back to them at the next session. You come to me, and I'll give you the answer. It's as simple as that."

I never realized teaching Greek would be so easy. Maybe next term I would teach a course in astrophysics or microbiology. And there was always poetry, another course in which I got a "C."

There I was, Life Guard in the Lake of Linguistics, without even a tenderfoot scout merit badge in swimming. What to do? First off, I confessed with total (Speech Clinic) honesty to the class of fifteen men seminarians exactly what I had told the Dean and what he had told me. I explained, "We'll be learning Greek together." I added one feature that saved the day. I assigned one major Greek word each week about which they would prepare a word study by Friday. These were major theological words like faith, sin, repentance, hope, hypocrisy, love, forgiveness, spirit, flesh, evil, etc. "Using a concordance and other helps, try to find out if these words are used differently by various of the Gospel writers and Saint Paul in his Epistles. You will find these key words, and others like them, coming up in the texts on which you will be preaching." They were enthusiastic to discover that Greek might have some practical usefulness. I suppose the school should have lost its accreditation, but I was already learning a lot about academe and enjoying the roller coaster ride.

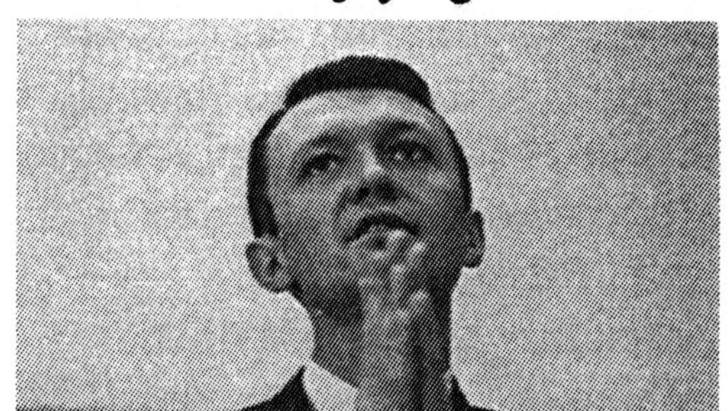

Some rascal in the front row of the Greek class snapped this photo of me. His caption translates into "I hear the angels." I submitted the photo together with my resume to a contest on sainthood, but it was rejected on the basis that no Norwegian could ever look that holy without being on some illegal drug.

Another task the Dean handed me was to serve as counselor to students, which included administering and interpreting to the students their scores on the Strong Vocational Interest Blank, the Guilford-Zimmerman Temperament Survey and the Minnesota Multiphasic Personality Inventory. These psychological tests were now standard in all seminaries of the denomination, and the poor Dean had tried to tack this onto his own load. His field was Old Testament and Hebrew. The one score he looked for carefully was the M-F (masculinity-femininity) scale on the MMPI. If a student's score leaned even slightly toward the "F" end of the scale, he urged that student to find a girlfriend or at least "be careful." The needy student might find himself invited to the Flack home to meet one of the cuter sorority sisters on campus at a cozy dinner. The Dean followed Saint Paul's example "to be all things to all men" (and of course women). It so happened the "F" factor picked up aspects such as nurturing, caring and sensitivity, which are actually needed by social workers, psychiatrists, counselors and pastors, the capacity to have empathy with another person. It did not necessarily imply sexual orientation, although it could. Remember this was in the era when girls played with dolls and boys with trucks. Women became nurses and school teachers and men became cowboys or engineers. The women's movement didn't have much momentum in 1955. Nor were women ordained in the Lutheran church in those days.

We did have women in the seminary, but they were mostly Methodists. One, in her late thirties, comes to mind in vivid memory. She began sending me notes which suggested the kind of transference that would have scared Freud right out of his pants. Sometimes a note would be signed "Eros" (Greek word for erotic love), sometimes "Agape" (Greek word for spiritual love motivated by grace). Some samples:

Dear Dr. Belgum: Out of appreciation I should write you. The psychological approach to my religious experience has got me straightened out and hitting toward the right goal. I thank you for your kind and helpful attitude in guidance. Sincerely, A_____

Dear Mr. President Eisenhower: This is not intended to alarm you in any way. It is merely to inform you of the New Reformation Movement that is sweeping the country … Faithfully yours, A_____

Excerpts from a two-page note:

Your Message for optional reading to the boys: (This is a product of your through transference in Liturgics on Oct. 8) … My Spirit has become attuned to that of Dr. Belgum's. I love him dearly. I've noticed that just let one of the boys start the reaction, Dr. Belgum gets hold of the thought process and carries them through to completion. It is then that I receive an outpouring of His Grace and know His will for my life … Remember the story in *Kings* of the queen coming before King Solomon? She admired him so thoroughly that she was left limp. Her remark was, "the half hath not been told." Dr. Belgum, I would say the same to you. I've been accepting your love all along without even knowing it … Now It's about time I repay. Man has risen up. I'm the debtor to Christ …. Love, A_____

This woman had an appointment with me for 2:00 p.m. the next day. I asked the Dean's secretary if she would please bring in some forms for me to sign at exactly 2:10 p.m. I told her I'd be having an appointment with A_____. Like so many secretaries, this one was a genius and highly sensitive to what might be going on. Sure enough, the woman client waxed ecstatic at our meeting and in a short while, like the Queen before King Solomon, she went limp and slid off her chair right onto the floor, her skirt all disarrayed. Just at that moment the Dean's secretary entered with the papers. I was so pleased not to be alone with the poor woman. The secretary phoned her husband, who came over right away and we were able to get her into the small psychiatric unit in the local hospital. Any time previous to this episode, I doubt if she would have consented to therapy since everything was cast in such religious dimensions and in her calling into the ministry. She got the help she needed. If there is ever one consistent feature about my career, it is this: One never stops learning from experience.

In that day, college faculty usually had the summer off to do with as they wished. The Lutherans of Michigan invited me to be the director of their summer youth camp near Kalamazoo, which is what I did for two summers. It was situated on beautiful and sizable Gun Lake, but it was crowded. Seventy kids and fifteen staff did it all on three acres with the long leg of the triangle on the beach front. What attracted me was the possibility of using this ten-week summer session as a group dynamics laboratory for college students from Wittenberg majoring in education, planning to be parish workers and Christian Education Directors. Several seminarians also took it for credit. During nap time, after lunch, we would meet to discuss what was going on, what should be going on and any problems among the campers. Each one wrote a special report in the form of a project/term paper. One seminarian developed a series of evening Vespers around the campfire. He drew inspiration from the coals of the fire, the sunset and clouds, reflections on the lake, sounds of the night, etc. Another taught about creation and nature in the great outdoor classroom and nature walks.

Naturally, there would be one exceedingly difficult camper. I'll call him Butch because that's what he was like--tough, hyper-active, very strong and macho, a problem to his parents and home community. Now it so happened that camp lasted a week, but one could sign up to stay over for a second week. Bozo here stayed

four weeks. I racked my brain about what to do with this bundle
of energy. I knew he liked to swim and to show off.

"Butch," I said, "would you do a really big favor for me?
You know how some kids just don't have any sense when it comes
to water safety. Joe, our lifeguard, is a great guy, but he can only
do so much. Would you be willing to help out as our Chief Outer
Limits Watch Patrol? Swim back and forth along the safety limit
rope and make sure no one goes beyond that line." And he did
that to a fare-thee-well, swimming like a submarine chaser during
each swimming period, meanwhile getting himself so exhausted
that he fell into bed and slept like a baby every night. Several
times I would make mention to the entire camp how fortunate we
were to have an Assistant Life Guard this year. We got along
fine.

Remember how I said stutterers were among the obsessive
compulsive crowd. I turned mine to good use. The camp, like
many voluntary agencies, was plagued with useless "gifts"--
broken down folding chairs, hymnals with covers missing, junk
that churches no longer could use. "Beware of Greeks bearing
gifts" was as true in the 1950s as in antiquity.

"How many of you campers enjoyed the Saturday night
campfires last year?" I asked one evening. All hands went up.

"How many would like a campfire every night?" Same
story.

Besides being compulsive I am a just-so-barely-controlled
pyromaniac and love campfires and to this day search for twigs to
burn in the garden. Needless to say, by the end of the summer
there was no more junk, scraps of this or that, not even a used
popsicle stick left on the grounds. If anyone would have asked if
we made good use of one of their assorted gifts, I could have
replied, "Yes, thank you, we used it during the evening Vesper

Service, and the children all enjoyed it so much. It was very inspirational."

In the spring of 1955 came a very great surprise and turning point. It was a tough decision precisely because everything was going so well in Springfield, Wittenberg and Hamma. It was there that my first book was finished, typed by the Dean's secretary on her time off--the transition of my dissertation into a textbook for seminarians and students of Clinical Pastoral Education in institutional settings. Knowing me as you now do, you understand why I was so elated when David Steere's book, *The Supervision of Pastoral Care,* came out thirty-three years later and said, "Perhaps the best single volume on supervision in clinical pastoral education is D. Belgum, *Clinical Training for Pastoral Care.*" Yes, things were going so well that the decision to leave was indeed difficult. The issue was an invitation from my Alma Mater; Northwestern Lutheran Theological Seminary, which had done so much for me, invited me to join their faculty in my own specialty and build a new program from scratch. The task combined six hours of teaching Pastoral Care and Counseling, Psychology of Religion, etc., per term together with counseling students and supervising their Field Work and Vicarage (a year's practicum in a parish prior to their senior year).

So, I went up to Minneapolis for an interview, which turned out to be every bit as pleasant and positive as my admissions interview ten years earlier. Wouldn't you know, Karl, our first-born, decided to arrive six weeks early (according to his novice parents' calculations) on May 12th, the day I was being interviewed in Minneapolis. Dean Flack visited Kathie in the hospital to extend his congratulations and blessing. To a nurse's query as to whether he was the father of the child, he, in his sixties, smilingly replied, "No, I'm not Abraham; I'm Dean Flack, a friend of the family." It was off to Minneapolis for eight-and-a-half years of rewarding experience in theological education. The folks at Wittenberg and Hamma were very gracious, saying they thought it was an appropriate opportunity for me and they wished us well.

Here is where Kathie's good financial judgment paid off. Out of her savings we had enough for a down payment on a modest but comfortable house in Richfield, a suburb south of the Seminary. She was a good sport about moving further from her family and toward mine, who were Twin Cities residents. I'll tell later in the story how our marriage was transformed into a more egalitarian teamwork, but for now she assumed the role of mother, homemaker and grocery shopper on Saturdays when she had full control of the car. She enjoyed singing in the Richfield Lutheran Senior Choir and making friends. It was only in retrospect that I realized how confining life in the suburbs with (finally) three small children could be. Like many men of that generation, it took me a while to become sensitive to women's issues. Before I say more about a great family, let me tell you of the opportunity and challenge that lay before me in Minneapolis.

I knew that there was an abundance of settings for clinical learning concerning people in need of pastoral care. The word clinic comes from the Greek meaning "pertaining to a sick bed." Thus clinical medicine is the next step in training beyond "basic sciences." The basic sciences in theology were biblical studies, church history, systematic theology and the like. My job description was to help the students put theory into practice. How can a pastor or chaplain help a patient draw upon his/her religious resources to deal with loneliness, despair, guilt, sorrow, anger, etc., the many moods and feelings that show up so often in the stressful lives of hospital patients? In fact, in a couple months in a major hospital, a student could encounter as many "problem cases" as would be met with in a small parish in many years. Here people are having limbs amputated, intractable pain, terminal illness, disabling conditions (some carrying stigma or shame), as well as the joys of recovery, giving birth to a healthy baby, finding remedies to long-standing maladies. In short, the hospital is a place symbolizing and concentrating the human condition in capsule form. Yes, Paul Johnson had been wise to find such laboratories in which to test out theories and practices of care and support.

In Minneapolis I gained access to the following institutions: University of Minnesota Hospital, Minneapolis General Hospital (now called Hennepin County Medical Center), Swedish Hospital, Saint Barnabas (Episcopal) and Methodist Hospital. To each center I sent four or five students in the role of chaplain (ecumenical, no proselytizing, naturally) to call on patients who otherwise had no one to call upon them. The Head Nurse usually pointed out patients she thought would benefit from a visit. In the case of Minneapolis General, owned by the City Board of Public Welfare, I cleared the program with that body. They asked if I had checked with the Catholic priest who came from a nearby parish, which I had done. He was delighted someone else would help fill the void in a large hospital, which can seem quite de-personalized to folks who may not have much social support in the first place. The students' visits were discussed in a debriefing session at the hospital. It all tied in with lectures and readings back in the Seminary classroom. I was glad to see all the hospitals welcoming this development. In both Minneapolis General and University hospitals, the Hennepin County Council of Churches created a full-time chaplaincy position; and finally the hospitals took greater initiative in integrating pastoral care into the total therapy program along with other specialties.

Each summer I conducted a 40-hour-per-week program of Clinical Pastoral Education in one or another hospital, first at General until they got a full-time chaplain and then at University until they had one also. By that time each had a fully accredited training center. All this was most gratifying. In fact I don't recall ever teaching a course in my career in which I did not consider both theory and practice as interrelated.

Since Clinical Pastoral Education (CPE) is a rather unique kind of education in theological circles, it bears a bit of explaining. In programs accredited nationally by the old Institute of Pastoral Care in those days, it was customary to immerse the students in hospital milieu and ethos by fulfilling the role of "orderly" or "attendant," wheeling patients to the operating room or physical therapy, observing surgery and other treatments, even helping in giving baths in selected cases--all under the supervision of a nurse. I also took them to the morgue to observe an autopsy. In other words, I wanted them dunked into the blood and guts of illness, as well as oriented to the many rules and policies that are necessary to run a complex hospital. I wanted them to get a glimpse of sickness behind the scenes. Maybe they would wrestle with the different meaning of two Greek words that are closely related and often confused: σαρχ (sarx) meaning flesh, sometimes translated as worldly as in temptations of the flesh, and σομα (soma) meaning body as in psychosomatic. Ah, back to the old Greek word study. How does the body affect the mind and spirit of a person--especially in brain damage, some endocrine imbalance or malformation of limb or organ? Is the body good, evil or neutral? The patient we call on in the bed is a body as well as a soul or spirit. We call it wholistic medicine. Even just being admitted to the hospital and forsaking one's civilian clothes and other symbols of identity and status can be traumatic enough. Does the student have the perspective to see hospitalization and treatment from the patient's point of view? Is the student willing to forsake preconceived ideas and judgmentalism, to shut up about his/her own interpretations and allow the patient to say what this or that means? Thus one gradually acquires the capacity to have empathy for another person, to be open to experiencing *with* the patient.

Here is an unsuspecting group of summer students outside Minneapolis General Hospital waiting to "be dunked into life and come up dripping," as Reuel Howe, a supervisor, put it.

Perhaps a way of showing what to do may be illustrated by a negative example. Years ago when a relative of mine had surgery in a large hospital, a retired Lutheran minister was routinely making the rounds of Lutheran patients representing an agency of the church. In the morning he would have his devotions and if five particular verses of Scripture were meaningful for him, then he would "administer" those words to the patients he would see that day. My relative said she could hear those verses coming down the hall, coming into her room and then receding down the other way along the hall. No provision if this or that patient might have a unique need. It reminded me of what I said earlier of the Bible being like a bottle of medicine. Just dip into it and apply like an ointment. We were now trying to be mindful of individual differences. Even pain tolerance is different among persons. Some are hopeful and not easily discouraged; others are almost constantly depressed and fearful. Some have a simple and confident faith in God; the next one is rebelling against anything and everybody including God. The great theological words we wrestled with in the Greek class at Hamma are assimilated differently by various persons. Hence, first we need to listen and try to sense where the patient is coming from, and then we are free to respond, to support, to say or do what seems appropriate. And then in the de-briefing session we can discuss it.

The other side of the coin is the personality of the student-chaplain. What hang-ups, prejudices, biases, strengths and weaknesses does he/she bring to the bedside? If he is terribly ashamed of his overweight mother or alcoholic father, it is not easy for him to approach a patient with one of these conditions with an open mind. The spirit may be willing, but the flesh says, "Yuch, not another one of those!" Many of us are not even aware how these subliminal messages speak to us: "Avoid this type."

"Now there's a really nice person." "Doesn't he have better sense than to smoke when he's just getting over lung surgery?" "How stupid, strong, wishy-washy, pleasant, etc., this person is." Time studies have shown that staff spend less time and make fewer contacts with patients of one kind over another. This comes from what is within the staff member, not from the objective need as recorded in the chart. But then, we are all human. It's just that if you are going to be in a helping profession, it is best to get rid of as many impediments in yourself as possible. Check all unnecessary baggage at the front door.

What makes this kind of educational enterprise so different from the behind-the-podium lecture method is the inevitable involvement of the instructor. In our small-group-dynamics sessions, sometimes called IPR groups (inter-personal relations), critique would be met by confrontation. As supervisor, I assured them they were free to point out my foibles as well as each other's. These became very open and honest sessions. After all, if we could not accept each other, warts and all, how could we relate helpfully to patients, who were also imperfect, even obnoxious at times? I got my comeuppance more than once. I never had a CPE group in thirty-three years in which I did not learn something about myself. It can be a bit embarrassing if you have to learn the same thing over and over again. We call that one a "slow learner." But then, please excuse me, remember I'm a Norwegian Lutheran in constant trouble in "thought, word, and deed."

The purpose of such a program is professional education, but there is often considerable therapy that takes place as a bonus --personal growth, self-acceptance (grace), feeling more comfortable with "all sorts and conditions," a lessened need for defensiveness, etc. One very rigid clergyman of about thirty years of age came to us in September so up-tight and agonizing with stomach ulcers that, when he went through the cafeteria line, it looked like it had snowed on his tray: mashed potatoes, cottage cheese, milk and vanilla ice cream. By Christmas he had let go of much unnecessary baggage, relaxed, become more open and honest, more accepting of himself and others. The ancients said it well: *Mens sano in corpore sano,* "A sound mind in a sound body." Sound, healthy thinking is better for us than neurotic thinking. It was gratifying to hear years later from former students who said CPE had been a big help to them in their ministry with the sick and dying, the troubled, the bereaved and many others they could mention.

But what does this digression have to do with the story of my life? I believe in many ways CPE sessions were a continuation and broadening of my Speech Clinic experience where I let go considerable excess baggage. But I doubt the job will be complete until I hear those words: "earth to earth, ashes to ashes, dust to dust" and feel the thunk on my bed covers three times. Then God will say, "Well done thou good and faithful servant. You sure aren't perfect, but I love you just the same." Then I'll say to Saint Peter, "Excuse me, I'm just passing by."

Yes, everything was peaches and cream at Northwestern; but sometimes the cream gets a little sour. The sour taste in the mouth of the faculty was some of the President's ideas about the curriculum. He wanted to teach The Gospel of John, and the faculty felt he was out of his field, which was actually church administration, polity, etc. He was a lawyer and had been a Synod President as well as pastor of a large church in Wisconsin. We figured academe was not his strong suit. (One might wonder why I should object to his teaching anything after my experience in the Greek arena at Hamma; but then, we are not always consistent.)

The part that was not good for our mental health was the fact that we grumbled about him and his ideas behind his back during coffee break and at our brown-bag lunches. I lacked some common sense when I brought home these frustrations and shared them at the dinner table when I should have been having a fun time with Kathie and the kids. Finally, I repented of my duplicity and poor judgment and made a simple decision. Instead of grousing, I would make a straightforward motion at the next faculty meeting stating why I thought it would not be a good idea for him to teach the John course. I would call for the question and accept whatever the vote was. The second part of my commitment was that I would not discuss it again. Issue closed! The faculty vote was negative. The president didn't seem that upset; after all, he had plenty of other fish to fry. Our family dinners were much more productive and positive after that. And again, I learned something.

The Family, In Minneapolis

Now I will relax awhile and tell about the really wonderful personal side of my life in Minneapolis. As you know, Karl was born just before we moved to Minneapolis, less than four months. The three children came fairly close together: Karl, May 12, 1955; Kurt, November 19, 1957; and Kit (Kirsten), April 28, 1959. I suppose there are advantages and disadvantages of spacing, sibling order, etc. It was quite different from my own family where we were born five years or more apart. The main thing was that our three children were all wanted and healthy and bright. What a blessing a wholesome family is when you look around and see the enormous amount of jealousy, abuse and just plain garbage in so many family relationships. Marriage and family problems seem so intractable in many cases, and I take my hat off to therapists who work creatively in this difficult field.

Maybe it was a good idea to have Sheba, the German shepherd, first so we could make any mistakes of parenting on her. You notice in the photo that Karl does not seem threatened by this big beast, but rather reaches over and pets her on the neck. Karl was born with a thick head of black hair and several furrows across his brow, like he was wondering if he'd make it into law school. Grandma Geigenmueller worried that having Kurt so soon would rob Karl of his childhood. We appreciated her concern, but not only was it too late to correct this error, but we really do not believe it damaged him in any noticeable way. He is now a partner in the law firm of Thelen, Marrin, Johnson and Bridges in San Francisco.

Kurt grew up to be the tallest of the family, at least two inches or more taller than I. Here he is at the age of five by our house in Richfield.

After a stint of high school teaching, Kurt went for a master's degree in applied linguistics at the University of Wisconsin and has been teaching English as a Second Language to foreign students at Georgia Institute of Technology. He and his wife, Gretchen, have two lively children.

The photo of "Kit," as Kirsten is called, indicates that she is obviously destined to be a professor of German Language and Literature at the University of Texas in Austin.

Her three years of study at the University in Freiburg have made her feel right at home in this field. Her second book will deal with German nationalism as revealed in popular literature of the last two hundred years. A very contemporary topic considering what is happening in eastern Europe.

Kathie and I have a lot of love and pride for these three healthy, well-established children of ours. They have been easy to rear.   The saying is that they enjoy coming back home summers for "quality deck time." As I reflect on their vocations, I note they are all in verbal careers: legal, linguistic and literary. "Little Caesar" would have been proud too.

The difference between my life as a husband and father in Minneapolis and what it had been a dozen years earlier, as a lonely bachelor lost in a dusty desert, would be like comparing day with night. I felt truly blessed as a secure and mature adult. I was pretty well keeping up with my goal of publishing a book every two years on the average, together with journal articles and an ample supply of speaking engagements here and there. Academe was a good life for me.

I shall return to this theme of wonderful family life in Chapter XIII, which deals with our life in Iowa City.

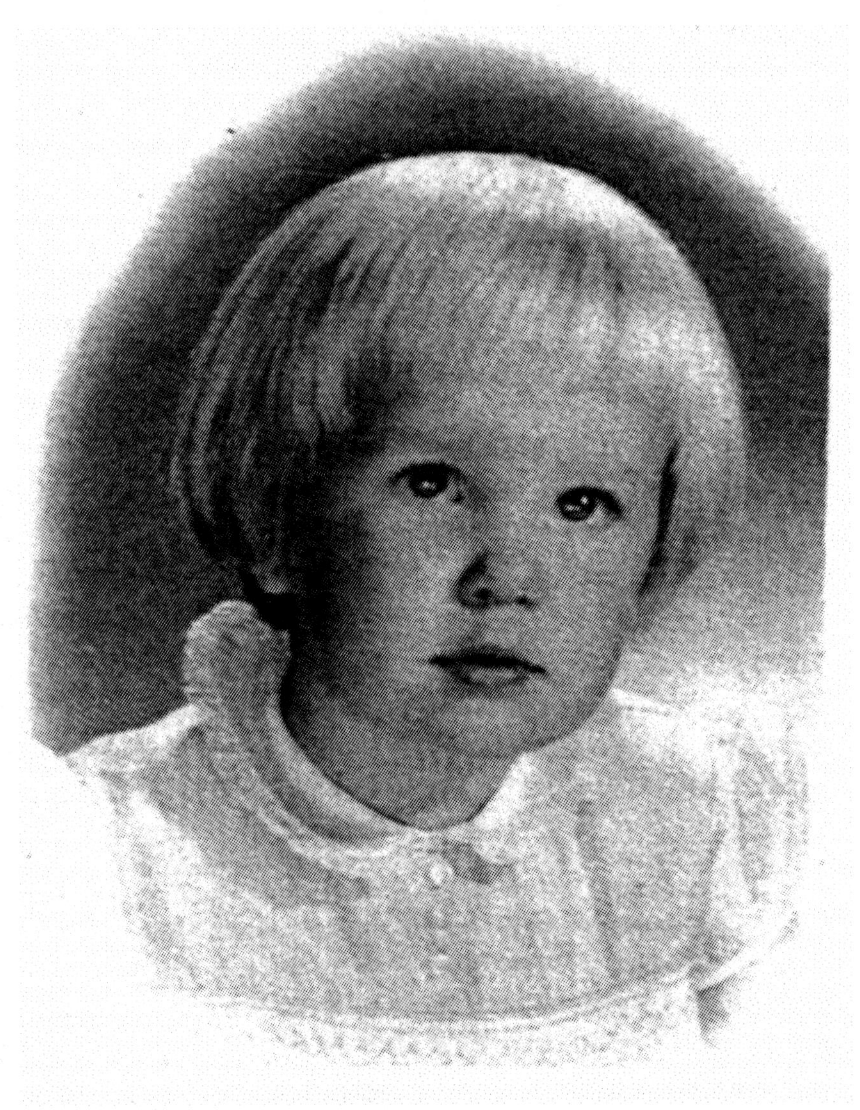

The image of this
blond little girl
speaks for itself.

CHAPTER XI

A SABBATICAL THAT REALLY PAID OFF

One of the perks of the academic life is the sabbatical leave of absence every six years or so. I was accepted as a Fellow in the Psychology Department of the University of Illinois under the Eli Lilly Endowment Program of Religion and Mental Health. The Seminary gave me the leave with full pay, and the generous stipend from the Endowment made the year very possible and comfortable. We brought along enough essentials for the nine months and found quarters in the Married Students' Housing complex where several other faculty on sabbaticals were also camping. Since it was temporary, the small quarters were quite acceptable. This was not far from the College of Agriculture research barns, so we took tours of the lambs, piglets, calves, etc. when they came into the world. Karl was in the first grade and Kurt attended Mrs. Samples' Nursery School. Kathie entertained Kit and generally managed the family while I did my thing.

Dr. O. Hobart Mowrer was generating a reputation in a new mode of counseling called "Integrity Therapy." The program was aimed at seminary professors of pastoral care and counseling--the other two men from a Baptist and a Dominican seminary in the San Francisco area. We were a most congenial group. We flew in a little six-seat airplane, belonging to the University, over to the Galesburg State Research Hospital.

There we would spend the day talking with psychotic, depressed women patients one-on-one and also in group meetings. Contrary to Freud's notion that people got sick from trying to be too good and repressing their Id drives, Mowrer believed many (not all) depressed patients had violated their Super-ego (conscience) and were punishing themselves with unhappiness under the assumption they did not deserve the "good life," normal satisfactions and fellowship with their loved ones.

Dr. Mowrer on the left, the Dominican on the right, heading for Galesburg. Continuous seminar on the way over and on the way back.

One case illustrating this point was rather dramatic. This middle aged woman from a small western Illinois community had been a local leader of 4-H, volunteered generously of her time and money, and had the reputation of being a model citizen. Mowrer suspected "guilty" people were bothered by this misplaced praise, and this seemed to be true in her case. Her "hidden life" was unsavory and, since she kept it "secret," there was no rehabilitation. This is certainly the theory of Christianity that sin unrepented of and unconfessed does not get forgiven, and the problem remains with the person, often repressed into the unconscious. When she "came clean" and admitted who she really was, not only to us in therapy group, but also to her husband, her depression lifted and she regained the capacity to enjoy life.

While I was in the program, two persons were referred to me for this kind of help. One was a farm wife so depressed she could hardly get out of bed to care for her children. She had been in and out of therapy and institutions, but to no avail. The conventional wisdom was that she was overly scrupulous and being burned out by her heavy responsibilities and over-conscientiousness (à la Freud). She finally admitted to me that she was ashamed about one thing. When her husband was gone and there were no customers at the grain elevators across the street, she would go over and have mutual masturbation with the elevator operator in secret. Mowrer's theory was that overwork might make a person exhausted or even drop in his/her tracks with fatigue but did not lead to neurosis. This woman had violated her covenant with her husband and society's social mores; and she had not been caught by the police, but by her own conscience, which had provided the punishment, which she later admitted she deserved.

I asked if she had shared this with her husband. "Oh, no! you see he is a big, strong man six feet tall." As a Lutheran church member, she evidently was more afraid of this man near-at-hand than she was of God the Father off somewhere. Or maybe God was a wimp compared with her big husband, a heresy to say the least. I asked her what she thought her husband was paying for her behavior--not able to go out socially, bowling, having friends in for dinner, etc. He had an incapacitated wife. I thought of the Scripture passage saying "He who eats and drinks (of the Lord's Supper) unworthily, eats and drinks to his/her own damnation." Why, yes! glossing over one's real self with a hypocritical self only rigidifies and entrenches the problem pushing it ever more deeply into the self. That is why I suggested to her that she may wish to delay receiving Communion or praying further to God until she had become reconciled to her husband. She said she would think it over. It was a whole new way of looking at religion as far as she was concerned (and maybe for many theologians as well). You see, it put a whole new twist on the secrecy of the confession. She was just about ready to replace hypocrisy with honesty. She decided to make the leap of faith and admit her aberration to the one who was most affected (omitting the other party's name--don't confess other people's sins). According to Mowrer there was little point becoming reconciled to a counselor, psychiatrist or priest with whom you had not been significantly related anyway, and then not to be reconciled to your most "significant other." To make a long story short, her depression lifted and people wondered what had come over her now that she had come out of her slump and shell. She had gained a new lease on life and reality was OK now.

Another case was a man who had contemplated suicide while sitting by the river for several hours. He had a combination of nonfunctional behaviors (if the term "sin" sounds too severe for you). He was an alcoholic and trying to hide it; and he had not been very honest about money (in connection with Illinois politics). When he broke out of hypocrisy and confessed honestly who he was, the road to recovery opened up for him. I accompanied him to his church, at his request, where he poured out his remorse in a torrent of words and tears. It reminded me of the scene where Jesus perceived there was an unclean spirit in a man. "And the unclean spirit, convulsing him and crying with a loud voice, came out of him." We went from there to his first Alcoholics Anonymous meeting. The big battle had been won; now there were just mopping-up operations. He went on to establish other AA units in surrounding towns, became a whole person as he replaced his old, destructive behavior with a new, constructive kind. He had regained his integrity. His relations with his wife and business partner son improved dramatically. His health also stabilized. I phoned him recently and his widow informed me that he had died a couple of months ago at the age of eighty, a long and fruitful life after coming so close to having a foreshortened and futile one.

One does not get involved with this kind of stuff without having some positive changes and new directions take shape in one's own life. I found this two-semester seminar-research sabbatical another stepping-stone in my own personal growth, to say nothing of a new professional perspective I could weave into my teaching and writing. The first book I completed on leave was entitled *Guilt: Where Religion and Psychology Meet,* published by Prentice-Hall. The other book that grew out of this sabbatical was also published by Prentice-Hall, *The Church and Its Ministry,* a synthesis of my psychology of religion and sociology of religion views. The representative of the publisher, who came down from Chicago to take me out to lunch and sign two contracts, made an interesting statement. "You know it is hazardous to publish a book," he said slyly, looking over his coffee cup to discern my reaction. "If your ideas are no good, many people all over the country will know about it. If you had not written the book, only a few students in your classes would know of your shortcomings." He continued with a smile, "On the other hand, if these are good ideas and helpful information, you will be appreciated. I think the latter in your case." My mother, hoping to reduce the temptation of the sin of pride, simply said of the two books, "My, that publishing house is sure good to you." It was the same remark she made when I got my doctorate from Boston University. Regardless, for myself, I thought this was a sabbatical that really paid off, two hardcover books in one year. This year built upon the other two therapeutic or growing experiences: the Speech Clinic and Clinical Pastoral Education.

To celebrate this successful sabbatical, Kathie and I decided to venture forth on an ambitious camping trip. We would head south to Little Giant State Park in southern Illinois. There we unfolded our new tent for the first time and realized we should have brought a hammer to drive the stakes into the hard ground.

As other campers watched me use a stone as a hammer, some took pity on us by sharing tools and know-how. They even suggested we could use what was left of their coals in their grill. We unrolled our bedrolls and tried to balance ourselves on assorted air mattresses. The trip was launched, alright!

Next it was on to Mammoth Cave Park in Kentucky, a great experience, and the kids were having a good time hollering into the caverns and hearing their echo return in waves. Gradually we worked our way north to Monroe, Michigan, for a visit with the folks and relatives and a few days at the cottage by Lake Erie. Now for the trek north, yes, really north. We crossed into Canada at Sault Ste. Marie, Ontario, and pressed on to Pancake Bay for our overnight campground. It looked great as the sun set brilliantly over the vast expanse of Lake Superior. We wrapped ourselves in our makeshift blanket rolls and nearly froze to death in August. At first light we rushed for the car and turned on the heater as soon as the engine warmed up. Then we peered through the windshield and noticed that the water left in a basin was frozen solid. Yes, it was cold with a brisk wind blowing off frigid Lake Superior. We continued our Great Circle Route around the lake and finally warmed up around Duluth. How good it felt to get into our cozy house in the Richfield suburb. It had been an adventure.

CHAPTER XII

BACK TO A PROLETARIAN STATE UNIVERSITY

The sabbatical at Illinois reminded me of how much I enjoyed the setting of a large state university, its diversity and interdisciplinary opportunities. Not that I was dissatisfied with my position or job description at Northwestern Seminary; there was just an intuitive sense that the university was my natural habitat. Maybe it was the ecumenical enjoyment I had developing the CPE program at the University of Minnesota Hospital. I invited the Catholic priest from a nearby parish, who served as part-time chaplain, to join me in a seminar for six of my students combined with six from Saint Paul (Catholic) Seminary down the river a mile or so. I had already cleared it with Professor O'Sullivan, who was my counterpart at that seminary. He thought it was a great idea. We would meet to get the assignments on which patients to call and then return for a seminar discussing the experiences and focusing in on one or two verbatim interviews from the previous week. Such a good spirit of fellowship developed that when time for ordination came around in the spring, each group invited the other to attend, and they all did: the Lutheran ordination in the impressive Mount Olivet church and the other at the Saint Paul Cathedral. That was back in 1963 before the ice had thawed elsewhere. Each group learned from each other in ways they had not expected and became friends.

I happened to know that our sister university to the south, in Iowa City, had the largest university-owned teaching hospital in the country. It also had the first academic department of religion of any state-owned university in the country. What a combination. I wrote to Bob Michaelsen, the Director of the School of Religion, inquiring whether they had ever been interested in a program of Religion and Medicine or Religion and Personality, a program that could bridge the two disciplines plus provide a clinical setting for study and research. He replied rather quickly indicating that, yes, they had just been discussing such a matter. They had inquired of leaders in the field, and O. Hobart Mowrer of Illinois had suggested they consider David Belgum. Here was handwriting on the wall again. I was invited for an interview with a variety of persons involved: Director of the Hospital, Dean of the College of Medicine, Head of the Department of Internal Medicine, Director of the School of Religion, Dean of the College of Liberal Arts and others involved in this kind of personnel selection. I was acceptable to all concerned, and I was very pleased about the visit. I began at the University of Iowa wearing several hats on March 1, 1964. I had professorial appointment in both the School of Religion in an area we decided to call "Religion and Personality," and a joint appointment in the College of Medicine. They also wanted me to create a department of pastoral services or chaplaincy in the hospital, which I could use as a clinical base, an official support program of CPE. Meanwhile, this would enhance the role of pastoral care of patients far from home, since the hospital served the entire state. For some time both the religious community and the hospital staff had wanted to upgrade and enlarge this service for the patients. They were killing several birds with one stone (or one hardheaded Norwegian). The job description with all its resources and connections suited me well.

From the beginning, I arranged that CPE should also be listed as a graduate course. Through the School of Religion, I was able to offer both M.A. and Ph.D. degree programs. Those who came only for one summer session and wished merely to use CPE as continuing education for their parish ministry were welcome to sign up for a category called "professional improvement." The university also used this category for practitioners in other fields such as accounting, education, etc. There was in place a very successful and comprehensive Extension Division with "continuing education" opportunities of many kinds. Among them were radio and correspondence courses, "distance learning" (where a professor went to some central point removed from campus), and "telebridge," a kind of conference phone-radio hook-up whereby a professor could relate to three or four sites connected with microphones and loudspeakers. By the time I had retired I had participated in all of these modalities offering courses for credit such as Religion and Personality, Death and Dying, and Medical Ethics. It was very gratifying because these nontraditional students were highly motivated, often acquiring degrees while working full-time. Years after a course thus offered, someone would say, "I enjoyed your course on the radio," or "Your course on Death and Dying meant so much to me because my mother was terminally ill at the time. Your lectures on 'grief work' helped me." Yes, I especially tried to apply theory to practice. If it does not work, it is not a good theory; and anything that works must have some theory to explain it, or so it seemed to me. My term of service to the University of Iowa was March 1, 1964 to December 31, 1987. At age 65 I decided there were two routes to retirement: Keep on till you don't enjoy it; or quit while you're ahead. I did the latter with a great deal of satisfaction and completion. After nice parties, congratulations and gifts, I did what I tell the recipients of Communion to do after the blessing at the altar rail: "Depart in Peace." I also told my successor, Dr. George Paterson, and his colleague, John Saeger, "I wish you all well, but I will not be hanging around getting in your way." George replied in his inimitable way, "Are we to construe that as benign absence?" "You've got it, George."

So how was it, getting started from scratch? It was a challenge. First off, I hoped to develop a good academic image of this new program. Just because it had to do with religion did not mean it would compromise with mediocrity. What this novice program needed was respect from other professors on both sides of the river, the humanities and the medical establishment. The reason I was asked to begin March 1 was to provide time to generate the first program in the summer of 1964. Get off to a good start! It was assumed that theological students and clergy interested in this program would all have completed their bachelor's degree at least and be clearly of graduate caliber. But I had to rely upon applicants. I had to sell the program by inviting applications.

Wouldn't you know it--one of the early applications for the summer of 1965 came from a farmer/minister who had some Bible College credit but no degree. It was common among the Mennonites to have their clergy rise up from their midst. Even the choice of a Bishop among them followed the practice used in the New Testament when Judas Iscariot, the betrayer, had to be replaced in the group of disciples. They drew lots. Nothing about grade-point average, I.Q., references, ACT or SAT or scores on nationally-respected entrance exams. Drawing lots! Gambling! To choose a bishop, candidates were to draw slips of paper from a closed Bible and the shortest, longest or something won. The Graduate College of the University of Iowa had never even considered such a method for admitting students, leave alone hiring faculty or promoting a person to the deanship. Suddenly, something drew me up short. One key to my program was going to be a broad ecumenicity. I had come to realize that not everyone even wanted to be a Norwegian Lutheran. In a state university one should be open to all "sorts and conditions." On top of that a large number of Mennonites from the colony about a dozen to twenty miles Southwest of Iowa City worked at University Hospital in a variety of positions from housekeeping to nursing. I turned to the provision for "professional improvement" and hoped for the best. The Rev. Dean Swartzendruber, age 38, had been ordained five years previously and served a sizable rural church, Lower Deer Creek Mennonite Church. It turned out he was the best student in the group: intelligent, well motivated to learn, open to new ideas, a nice combination of self-confidence and humility. He formed meaningful relations with the patients and was respected and appreciated by the staff. It scared me to think how close I came to allowing purist elitism to cloud my thinking. Over the years I continued to form many fine relationships with the Mennonites, speaking or preaching in five or six of their churches and conducting a series for their clergy. As I said before, I continued to learn from experience. Two of our better graduate students earning Ph.D. degrees, John Hershberger and Lonnie Yoder, were also from this tradition, and I preached the ordination sermon for John at First Mennonite Church in Iowa City.

What a mix we had over the years, old and young, men and women, Catholic, Unitarian, Missouri Synod Lutherans, Presbyterians, Seventh Day Adventists, Re-organized Latter Day Saints, Baptists, Episcopalians, a Rabbi and you name it. I recall monks from at least three orders: Dominican, Norbertine and Trappist, and nuns from Chicago, Iowa and Trinidad. We had students from Iceland, Papua New Guinea, Canada and Europe. There were also lay people. After all, in a state university, you could hardly list ordination as a requirement to get into a class. Now there are also many openings for lay persons to serve in religious vocations in chaplaincy posts and as what is called "Associate in Ministry." A graduate program in counseling across the river listed our program as one of the options in which to serve a practicum for clinical experience. The reason that such immense diversity worked well was that we did not sit around focusing on our differences, but concentrated on the needs of the patient under consideration. How could we stand by this patient as he/she wrestled with some issue of medical ethics or life/death choice, mustered the courage and energy to enter upon vigorous physical therapy and rehabilitation, and dealt with values and meaning of his/her life? It was great and always rewarding. We all learned from each other how to become more helpful care givers.

In the late '60s and '70s there was the tremendous push for equality, participatory democracy on campus, de-emphasis on status, etc. I agreed with much of this but occasionally took the opportunity to put things into perspective. In one of our group dynamics sessions, several doubted if I was truly a member of the "group" or felt set apart as the leader. There was a fearful dread of authoritarianism, and often rightfully so since HERR PASTOR had often lorded it over the laity. After one such confrontation, I couldn't help myself. I said, "I agree that under God we are surely all equals. In fact the only difference between me and the rest of the group is that I get a salary and you pay tuition." One strong voice softened and said with a smile, "Yes, and I guess you are the only one whose signature the Registrar will honor." That broke the ice. In fact, often humor and teasing would be interspersed with very heavy discussion. Each group was different and stimulating in its own way--some more stressful than others.

Meanwhile, as a professor I wrote books and journal articles in a way that suited me. I never wrote anything in order to get promoted. An idea or interest would ferment for a while. Maybe I would speak on it at some group to which I had been invited (field testing the idea). If it seemed to pertain to the needs

of patients or hospital staff, it might grow into a course, like my
Seminar on Stigma, which in turn grew into a book mentioned
above. By this time in my career I reflected on what role
stuttering had played in my life and I drew the following chart
(beginning at nine o'clock, follow it clockwise).

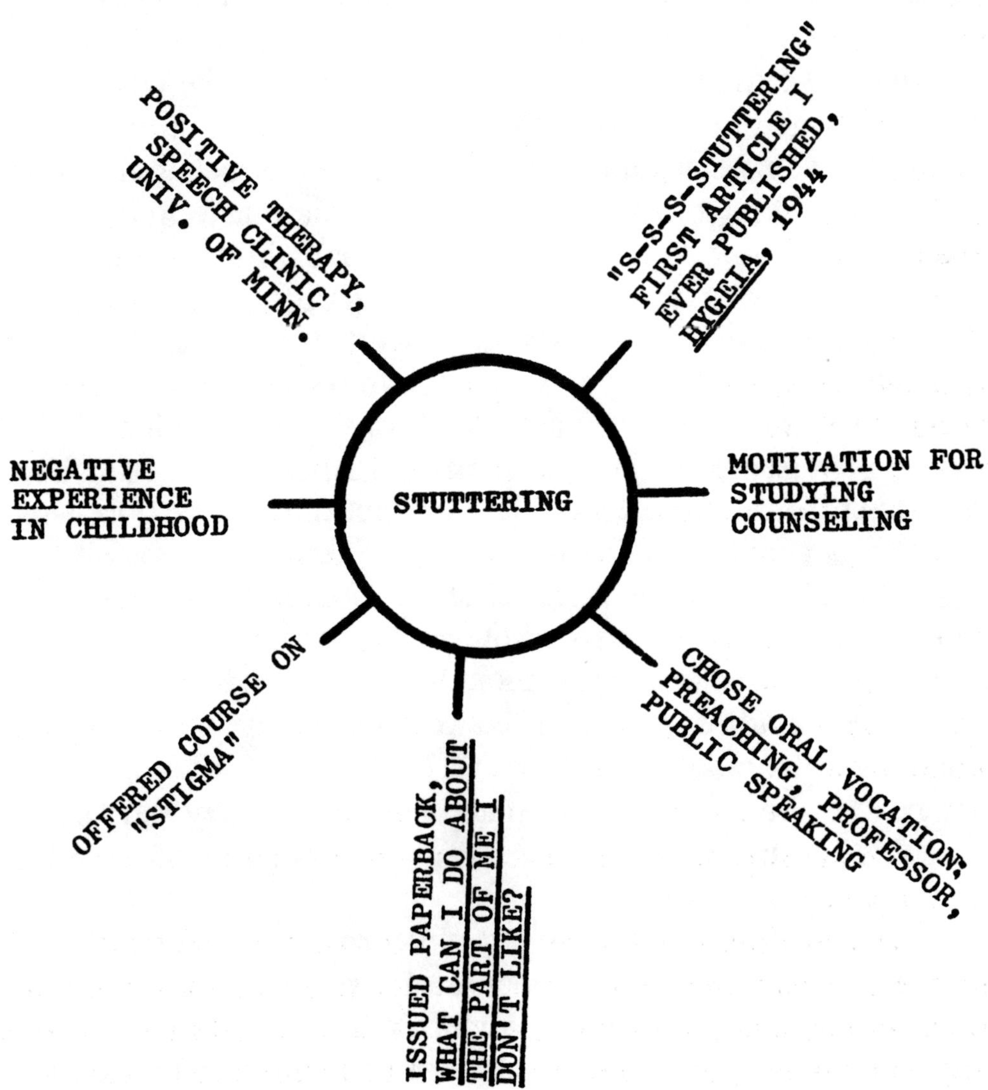

Ramifications of Stuttering

My largest class, about 250, was Death and Dying. It began as a small seminar for graduate nursing students. After it got under way, Elizabeth Kübler-Ross had a spectacular article in *Life* magazine on her work with terminal patients at Billings Hospital, University of Chicago. She had agreed to come and her article appeared two days before the class session at which she was to lecture. The attendance that night jumped from 35 to 200 with students sitting in the aisle. She popularized the whole field of the study and therapy of dying persons. When I threw the class open to undergraduates, the attendance skyrocketed. Then it was also carried over the University radio station, WSUI, broadcast from one of the largest lecture halls in the medical center. As a correspondence course, it averaged about sixty enrollees, a steady stream. My first effort to consider the dynamics of dying and grief went back to the time I was asked to preach on all of the Seven Last Words of Christ at a Good Friday Service in Wisconsin. The publisher, Al Anderson of Augsburg Publishing House, teased me, "It's the first time we've published a chapter as a book"--*His Death and Ours*, 1958.

One of the joys of working at the University of Iowa was the open attitude on the part of the administration, department heads and business managers, including the Iowa Foundation. Whenever I would suggest I'd like to do something, like offer a course over the radio, they'd say, "That's fine; go ahead." If I may be excused a self-serving statement, maybe they were so agreeable because what I suggested worked in terms of attendance and money, etc.

One venture I was ashamed of because it failed totally in my view. I had prepared a brochure for raising funds through the Iowa Foundation for the Clinical Pastoral Education Program (stipends for students). The back page had endorsements by the President of the University, the Dean of the College of Medicine and the Director of the School of Religion. I sent out a very large mailing and received back not quite enough to cover the postage. I showed up at the Foundation doorstep ready to be chewed out for getting in over my head. The Foundation folks simply said, "That'll happen, but don't worry. You've planted the seed. We'll see what happens." Then during a luncheon for granting an award to a student, a wealthy businessman from Washington, D.C., was seated by me. I told him about the book I'd edited and recently had published by Iowa State University Press, *Religion and Medicine: Essays on Meaning, Values and Health.* He asked for a copy when he was back in Washington. He liked it and asked for another copy for his pastor. Then when he became ill, he would call me from his hospital room and I would carry on pastoral care long distance. Finally, the man died; and when his will was read, there was $50,000 for the CPE Fund at The University of Iowa Foundation. Support came in from here and there and the program grew.

Another development or project that grew out of my chaplaincy role and seminar on death was the suggestion to the Anatomy Department that we should have a Memorial Service for the cremated remains of those who had deeded their bodies for study and research (like the Gross Anatomy class, which needed cadavers for dissection). They welcomed the idea and said, "That's fine; go ahead." Each first Friday in June we would meet at a cemetery lot Iowa City had donated for this purpose. Sometimes almost 300 family members and friends would attend, and it seemed to meet a need for closure. One year they came from eight states. I asked the CPE students to attend and mingle with the crowd in case some needed a shoulder to cry on or wished to chat about what this committal service was meaning to them. Some faculty and medical students also attended. A journal article grew out of that experience. The two following photos are from the scene of burial. I am casting soil on the common grave with the words, "earth to earth, ashes to ashes, dust to dust," commonly used by so many traditions at the grave-side ceremony.

Memorial
Grave Stone

Officiating at
Memorial Service

After teaching Religion and Personality for umpteen years, I decided to collect and systematize my own thoughts on the subject in the form of the inevitable textbook; this one, *Religion and Personality in the Spiral of Life,* was published by University Press of America in 1979 (enlarged edition, 1988). It also became a radio course and a correspondence course. Like my other books, this one has pretty well sold out. Most are out of print, which means the publisher is not out anything by having a lot of remainders left in the warehouse. At least that's one guilt trip I'm spared.

Believe me, the campuses throughout the country were more than places for lectures and football games in the '60s and early '70s. Flower children and anti-Vietnam War rallies and general antiestablishment sentiment characterized that period. "Tune in, turn on, tune out," or something to that effect. Let the drug culture waft you away to new heights of self-awareness. I performed a wedding at a farmhouse where Grinnell College students had a miniature commune. "Let it all hang out." "Make love not war." It went on and on.

In 1972 Augsburg Publishing House issued my little book, *Why Marry? Since You Don't Need a License to Love.* It contained, among satire, humor and seriousness, a "Why Q Test" and a "Discuss-O-Chart." I was amazed at how many speaking engagements this led to. I was glad a Canadian seminary student paper published the chapter left out by Augsburg. It was "Youth Bring Court Action," "Establishment Up for Heresy Trial." I thought it was clever beyond words.

Sometimes the rebellion got violent. One of our temporary class and office buildings was burned to the ground together with a few theses and who knows what all. There were sit-ins. Once when President Bowen was leaving to attend a camp retreat, where students, faculty and administrators were going to have a chance for open dialogue, a group of students climbed all over his car screaming that he never talked to students. In later days it got so tense that a call went out for faculty to walk, patrol and generally be available for defusing dialogue with students in dormitories. My watch was the Quadrangle Dormitory. Four of us just casually walked about and chatted with anyone who wanted to talk, argue or blow off steam. We were supposed to bridge the generation gap and let the students know there were adults who were willing to hear what they had to say and to try to understand, as the saying went, "where they were coming from." It was a tense night. Would the dorm be torched? Would a mob scene form and march downtown to break out some more store windows? There was no violence at that time, and I like to think we had a part in easing the tension--not solving anything, just providing a safety valve. It felt good.

To demonstrate that we faculty were not horrid fascist types like many in the establishment, many of us wore peace ties and beards. This sketch of me shows that I am a respectable double for Trotsky. Surely the students could not mistake me for the enemy, a clean-shaven member of the Fortune 500. There were many games and almost no one to keep score.

I spoke at various war moratoriums because I believed we had interceded in a strange way not commensurate with our own history. What if Spain had intervened when we wanted to elect George Washington, our emancipator and Father of His Country? That would have been awful. Ho Chi Minh, like Washington, drove out a colonial power from his land. For this he was considered the Father of His Country. Yet President Eisenhower claimed there should not be an election because Ho Chi Minh would obviously be elected to govern the country freed from French Colonial rule, like we were freed from British Colonial

rule. I may have been naive, but I was definitely against the war.
But it was finally over and things went back to normal.

It takes so many kinds of people to make up a well-rounded
major university. There are professors of fourteenth century
Portuguese literature, slipped disc surgery, Greek, electrical
engineering, creative writing, psychiatry, mathematics,
philosophy, quantum physics, social work, dentistry, etc. The list
is endless and growing all the time as new fields open up and old
fields close up either from lack of interest or money. Some
scholars are skilled at basic research and pioneer in medical

breakthroughs or a spectacular economic theory that will rescue our country from recession. Others are more of the applied type who teach how to put together a country town newspaper or how to "do" this or that. At our university a person can earn a very advanced degree by writing an excellent novel or creating a remarkable art piece (in fact Iowa pioneered in this kind of graduate study in which a person creates something rather than critique what someone else has created).

Unfortunately it so happens that a person adept at theoretical research may look down upon another whose job is to put theory into practice, like applying sociology and psychology to the profession of social work. One teaches music theory, another trains a student to become a gifted performer on the pipe organ. It is ideal when everyone can appreciate vocations which are quite different from one's own. For myself, I was never a great theoretician, and you will not find me quoted among creators of new theories of behavior or personality. Like Papa said about sermon preparation, "I milked many cows but the butter is all my own." You will recall my sabbatical study of guilt. I am also concerned about the dynamic of self-esteem. Last spring (1992), I published an article in the *Journal of Religion and Health* entitled "Guilt and/or Self-esteem as Consequences of Religion." It is the only time I have received requests for reprints from eight countries and numerous universities and therapists in the United States. It evidently struck a nerve, the juxtaposition of these two factors. I was trying to apply theory to practice. When I was asked to give a lecture at School of the Ozarks on the medical ethics of the Nancy Cruzan case, I entitled the article that came out of it, "The Right To Die at the End of Your Life." It was a complex of research by others plus my own clinical experience in hospitals with dying patients and the Death and Dying course. From that little talk grew seventeen requests to speak on the subject and an Opinion Page editorial in the *Des Moines Register*. Some downplay this type of contribution as simply "popularization," or "pop psychology." I accept that role and have enjoyed it; actually I found it very rewarding.

Our University Library includes, among its many special collections, a depository of practically everything any of the University of Iowa professors or scientists have written, books, journal articles, book reviews, speeches, etc. I have been glad for this service because it is easy for stuff to just plain get lost. I do not own several of my books, which are out of print. One keeps on lending and giving them away, including the last one. When you die, what interest do your descendants have in a project you completed fifty years ago or a book that went out of print forty years ago? Mostly, disposing of a professor's files is a puzzle and a chore. But anyone who would like to trace something he/she accomplished can find it in one secure, safe place, Special Collections.

Speaking of descendants, I should like to take time out again to refer to my family and what family life was like in the university town of Iowa City.

CHAPTER XIII

THE FAMILY AGAIN

Iowa City is a great place in which to raise a family. We lived two blocks from the football stadium and four from the Field House with its swimming pool, handball courts and basketball. Tennis courts, indoor or outdoor, half way in between. People come here, or come back here, to retire because of all the plays, concerts and other interesting events. It is true of any university or college town.

Our older son, Karl, elected to enter University School at the Junior High level. I, worrying still about the sin of pride, wondered if going to a "special" school would tempt him to elitism or snobbishness. Across the Cardinal restaurant in the old Jefferson Hotel, Howard Jones, Dean of the College of Education was sitting alone, waiting for his dessert. I asked if I might join him with my dessert. I popped the question. His reply was folksy but sound. "As far as I have observed, anyone at University School who was snobbish had brought it from home." Karl, as a law partner, is still not snobbish. But if we parents didn't worry, who would? I was pleased to learn that one of his friends from the neighborhood was Bobby Vedepo, son of a barber. The school tried to balance the disproportionate number of children of academics by a smattering of local farm children.

In those halcyon days of freedom and everyone doing one's own thing, University School was in the lead. In a chemistry class, Karl was mixing rocket fuel. It was great fun to shoot a rocket into the air and let the little parachute float it down again. How high could one make it go in the days when "Sputnik" spurred on young minds? He mixed ingredients A and B together, with mortar and pestle, when actually they should have

been ground separately and then combined. BANG! It blew up
in his hand, cutting him in several places. Kathie took him to the
excellent hand surgeon, Dr. Flatt, at the University Hospital
Emergency Room. The hand was quickly stitched, but the doctor
was more worried about Karl's eyes since his face was a bit pock
marked. His eyes were properly washed out and treated.
Fortunately he suffered no permanent bad effects. But the
theory-and-practice pair again emerged. Maybe not every bit of
knowledge should be acquired through "learning by doing,"
which progressives found so useful for many kinds of learning.
In Chemistry one could learn from lecture and the experience of
earlier scientists. Everyone does not need to learn to re-invent
the wheel from scratch, or discover that water runs down hill, or
learn that arteries carry one kind of blood and veins another. In
1983 we had the happy privilege of having Karl living with us for
a semester while he was on leave from his New York law firm.
He was teaching two courses as Visiting Professor at the
University of Iowa College of Law. They were Civil Procedure
and Environmental Law. He was well received by his students
and by us. Karl grew up in what was in many ways a chaotic
time, but he made it just fine.

In grade school Kurt was diagnosed as having trouble
saying his "r's" plainly; so, naturally, it was off to the Speech
Clinic after school for remedial speaking. He loved it and
attended faithfully. When Kathie and I had a visit with his cute,
blond therapist, we understood why he was so drawn to those
sessions. Now he helps Japanese, Chinese, Venezuelans, Russians
and an assortment of other foreign students learn to read, write,
hear, pronounce and comprehend English as a Second Language
(r's and all) at Georgia Institute of Technology in Atlanta. Kurt
especially enjoyed the sports facilities so close at hand and still
plays tennis and an assortment of games with racquets as well as

swims with his family. His four years at Luther College in
Decorah, Iowa (home of the Nordic Fest), may have preserved as
much Norwegian influence in his personality as anyone in the
family (myself excepted, of course).

It has become a ritual in our family reunions in the summer
time, in Iowa City, that Karl, Kurt and I play a round of golf. It
is a joy to continue such close relations with these two mature and
successful sons. Parenting has had its ups and downs in the past
few decades. It has swung like a pendulum from permissiveness
to dialoguing, to assertiveness to "tough love." Books on what
one must do, and what one must avoid at all costs, are coming off
the presses like Niagara Falls. Usually, parents end up with a
heavy load of guilt if their kids go awry or astray or afar or
aberrant. If one reflects on parenting as I have, one is sure to
find lack of guidance, over-bearingness, smothering and/or
aloofness enough to keep one on the mourners' bench during most
of the service. Case in point: One bright fall day, I made it a
point to come home early from the campus. Enough of helping
others in the hospital or the counseling room; it was time to
"parent" my sons for a change. Wouldn't they be appreciative to
see me seek out their fellowship so early on an ordinary
Wednesday for no special reason other than just wanting to be
with them! When I got home I could not find either one. They
were making use of the after-school and before-dinner time to be
with their friends, to play ball or whatever. They were totally
unavailable for "parenting" at that time. I forget what profound
meaning I found in this non event.

Kirsten Louise was the one child whose nickname stuck
until this very day when she is a professor. It was "Kit." Even
when she was a star swimmer in high school, coming in second in
the butterfly in the state meet at Fort Dodge, she was called
"Killer Kit" because of her competitiveness. She not only won

many medals and ribbons but made many good friends through the Iowa City Swim Club and through the school swim teams. They still keep in touch. And she still enjoys swimming recreationally and for fitness.

To all three, Kathie and I had said we would gladly pay for their college education equivalent to what in-state tuition, board and room would be at any of the three state universities in Iowa. Wouldn't you know, they all chose something else, and then, of course, earned the difference themselves in summers, etc. Karl took a bus to Madison, Wisconsin, and was sold on that institution for him. Kurt drove his Dodge Dart up to Decorah, maybe partly because there was beginning to be a small stream of students from Iowa City opting for that school. To show how times change: not only was he put in a guest house, but some students inquired if he wouldn't like to stay over Saturday night for the dance? Did I hear correctly, THE DANCE? AT A NORWEGIAN LUTHERAN CHURCH COLLEGE? It was also not as Norwegian as in the days when my father or older brother, Harold, went there--when it was totally and belligerently NON CO-ED. Blacks were being recruited to attend Luther and there were many progressive features, like Junior-Year-Abroad. Kurt spent the year in the University of Freiburg (im Breisgau). He was disappointed they put him with an American who did not speak German. He found employment on a farm high up in the Black Forest where hardly anyone had met an American in their life, even in the War. We were quite content and pleased that they each chose their own way.

Getting back to Kit, I had noticed how well she did in math and science courses. Was she headed toward engineering? Since I had offered (and followed it up) to take the boys on a tour of a couple campuses if they wished, the same went for Kit. We had an appointment at Ames, Iowa, with a professor of engineering who had formerly taught at Iowa. Iowa State University had a strong science and engineering reputation and, I thought, a very attractive campus. On each table in the Union Dining Room was a vase with cut flowers from their endless horticulture greenhouses. It gave her something to think about, but she chose Saint Olaf. She developed an interest in German and lived her sophomore year in das Deutsch Haus where German was spoken at meals and German folk songs sung sometimes in the evening. (The college also had special living houses for students majoring in French and Spanish.)

Toward the middle of her second year, she began to feel Saint Olaf was parochial, and maybe it was, compared with Iowa City. Anyway Kathie and I had a visit to Minneapolis, the route to which went right by Saint Olaf. "We'll meet you for dinner while we're passing by." "Fine," she replied, "I'll be studying in the Library, so hunt me up there." We parked and sought out our daughter, who should be easily recognizable with blond hair and her blue parka jacket slung over the back of her chair. We saw a veritable sea of blond Scandinavian girls with blue parka jackets slung over the backs of their chairs. Our first words to her, after "It's good to see you looking so well," were these: "We understand what you mean about so many all the same." She went to visit Freiburg in the summer and one day walked across the street to enroll at the University of Freiburg. She gave us a proposition we could not refuse: "Since there is no tuition here at this state university, you can afford to fly me home for Christmas." Parents do as they are told; so we did. A strange twist of academe is this: After three years at Freiburg she passed her *zwischenprufung* (loosely translated, "now that you have proven yourself to be between two categories, you are free to enter upon graduate work"). (Excuse me, Kit, I did the best I could.) This was more than an American bachelor's degree, nearer a master's, because the University of Wisconsin admitted her directly to the Ph.D. program in German Language and Literature. I was relieved when she received that diploma and I had it framed for her. After all, without it she would have had no degree at all and would not even have been licensed to teach German in Junior High.

In short they all sought out their own route and one that suited them well. Kathie and I were smart to leave hands off like Papa and Mama had done with me and my siblings.

As a family we developed traditions like Christmas get-togethers, the "deck time," golf, summer reunions, etc. The three planted a Colorado Blue Spruce on our twenty-fifth anniversary halfway between the house and the front sidewalk. Now it is about thirty feet tall at least, and in five more years will touch the house and sidewalk if not trimmed back gently.

Kathie had the idea of a major camping trip. Our first well-planned camping trip (in contrast to the one after the sabbatical in Illinois) was to the World Expo in Montreal, a great success. The campgrounds by the Saint Lawrence River were laid out as orderly as a motel, with each nicely landscaped lot numbered like a room in a corridor. The Expo was highly educational, with pavilions from numerous countries, international food cafes and exhibits of the latest technology and culture developments. Both Kathie and I thought such extended times apart just for family adventure and togetherness were very useful and refreshing.

Great Family Outings

Did I just now say "Kathie had the idea?" Yes, that was and is her forte. I love parties and special events, but it is Kathie who comes up with the ideas and they are always right on target. Oh,

I've had a couple good ideas in our forty years of marriage; but by and large it is she who makes out the guest list for football barbecues on the back deck, dinner parties, etc. It's like with the money, each one does what he/she can do best.

One of her excellent ideas was that we have a special family bash celebrating our wedding anniversary every five years. Our twenty-fifth was a family trip to the Black Hills, South Dakota, to Custer State Park. There we found a fascinating place to stay. There was a teacherage, a sizable apartment attached to the back of a remote country schoolhouse, which we were able to rent for the week. One morning several buffaloes ambled past our back door grazing on the lawn and looking at us like they were about to collect a fee for parking on their territory. Climbing Mount Harney, visiting the giant carving of the four presidents at Mount Rushmore, hiking and riding in a land-rover type vehicle to observe wildlife, herds and flocks; all this was enjoyed by all of us. We have always been a very congenial family when it comes to camping, outings, and plans.

In 1983 it was my turn to come up with an idea. We rented a houseboat near Clinton, Iowa, from a place called "Rent-a-Cruise." The boat slept, seated and comfortably housed eight persons. There were eight cups, plates, chairs, beds; everything furnished. I, as the Captain naturally, was taken out for a one-hour navigational instruction period and then set loose to go upstream to Dubuque and back again in four days and nights. I really paid attention because it was a very heavy boat and would not stop on a dime, as we learned later when the family following us smashed into the first lock at Clinton going North. The gracefully pointed bow of their boat now looked like a step ladder that had just been folded up ready to hang in the garage. The banks on both sides of the Mississippi were totally natural, not a barn, fence or cottage in sight because on the one side was a nature preserve and on the other a military reservation. At night we were told to find a sandy beach, head inland with enough speed to be securely beached and throw out an anchor on either side securing us for the night. It was also exciting to hear and see a big barge group pushed by a tug coming around the bend. Its light would flash back and forth regularly looking for markers and buoys as we had done earlier by daylight. The pace was slowed way down, and there was that relaxation which allows people to get caught up on each other in an unhurried way.

Now it was Kathie's turn to return to an earlier love, horses. For our thirty-fifth anniversary outing, she chose North Fork Ranch on a bubbly river that bounced and flashed over rocks, high up, not far from the Continental Divide in mid-Colorado. What a setting, mountains rising from the river valley. There was a stone bridge which we crossed to go from the dining hall and stable area over to our stone house, which we had all to ourselves. It had been built by a wealthy person years before and had its own hot tub. Kathie and Kit owned their own horses on our little forty-acre spread south of Iowa City about nine miles. For myself, I usually stayed away from horses the length of a pitchfork and have saved myself thousands of dollars of orthopaedic surgery by that simple device.

What should I do about these death-dealing beasts? I could stay in camp and read a good book. I could go hiking in search of an unspotted owl or a spotted deer. As I saw how level the paddock was and how authoritatively the wranglers spoke and acted around these circus animals, my fears subsided. Sunday they would just take a walk around and introduce each person to his/her horse for the week. I foolishly and carelessly thought there would be no harm in just taking this little orientation walk on a horse, who might be bored by this time in the summer. I even think I checked to see if they were covered with hoof

insurance. So off we went for a short ride, and it was a breeze.
But enough of that! Then Satan entered into the heart of the
owner of the Ranch. He announced with a straight face that
Monday morning there would be a Champagne Breakfast Ride.
Then Satan spoke softly to me just over my right shoulder (where
he usually sits in my case), "You didn't come over a thousand
miles to miss out on a Champagne Breakfast, did you?" "No, of
course not," I said, yielding to temptation, as we so often do in
this life. The ride began innocently enough exiting from the
paddock area out into nature--how pleasant. Once we crossed the
otherwise picturesque stone bridge, which I was glad my horse
did not fall off, we began to ascend, ever so seductively up a
smaller and narrower stone path. Finally the otherwise lovely
river was three hundred feet straight down to the rocks I had so
admired only yesterday, the last day of my life. At last we broke
out into one lovely and peaceful valley after the other with distant
vistas of the Colorado lower lands below. There we were within
sight of the cooks' pickup truck. The gourmet breakfast was
about to begin. And there were seconds on the champagne. It
was when we began heading down that I realized why they served
so much champagne. One needed to be half-conscious to risk the
tortuous descent down the same damn trail, even narrower now
than when we had come up. For a fleeting moment I thought of
offering to do the dishes if I could ride down in the back of the
truck, but I dreaded having to read in the corner by myself and
having no one speak to me the rest of the week. I had made it,
and Kathie said she was proud of me, as did horsewoman Kit.
The next trip I took up into high country was in a caravan of
several Jeeps for a tour of wildlife and gorgeous scenery. We
bounced fairly dangerously over enormous rocks and gullies, but
I feared no evil. The Jeep was made by intelligent engineers in a

modern factory; that horse had just been made by God. I have
never confessed this thought until this very sentence.

Kathie Wife and Companion

I must say a word about how my favorite nickname for
Kathie came about. In 1963, perhaps in gratitude for ten years of
good marriage, I dedicated a book to her thus: "To Kathie, Wife
and Companion." This became shortened almost to one word,
Kathiewife; and she still knows exactly what I mean when I use it.

Kathie and I have been a great pair these almost forty
years. We supplement each other in temperament and style. She
is skilled at seeing matters that need tending to, no doubt why she
is a very good Executive Librarian of the College of Law on
campus. She can organize things in sequence, as she says, "to get
the job done." My approach may appear more relaxed but I do
have my obsessive-compulsive streak, which also means I tend to
finish what I start whether it be a book (I've aimed at one every
two years) or a project in the house or yard. I made the drawings
for our bedroom addition off the living room, which were
accepted by our contractor in toto, with one caveat, "Is this line
the outside or inside of the wall" (difference of six inches). "I
stand corrected." Also, the extension to our deck for the growing
football crowd was executed as I planned.

Kathie has always been very supportive of me in many
ways, for example, co-operating with my vocational moves,
sabbaticals, journeys and speaking engagements. But is not the
giddy kind. She resembles her father in this. For example, in a
Christmas card, she wrote, "He has written several short stories
for 'fun,' which he evaluates much more highly than other
readers." She can be insightfully objective.

Our marriage roles changed considerably over the years. It is so important in change that both members of the partnership adjust to change, otherwise, like a square dance, you drift apart. When I first met Kathie in the context of her family, I thought, "This is great. Herr Vater sits at the head of the table with authority and respect. His work is his business. Mother makes the meals, runs the household and entertains guests, and does not ask questions about the Monroe Steel Castings Company." There was certainly no talk like the parsonage evaluation where it could be heard, "She is such a help to him in his work; he couldn't do it without her." In a German household there is a lot of status attributed to the father and his role is clear.

After we moved to Iowa City, Kathie found herself with a modified empty nest when Kit stayed at school through the lunch hour. She became bored with trying to fill her day with golf and coffeeing and busywork. Down at the Public Library, Kathie had been leading a Junior Great Books Club discussion group for 5th graders. When the University established a School of Library Science, Kathie got in on the ground floor and enrolled for the master's degree program, which she took on a half-time basis, still saving time for the kids when they returned from school. Her first vocation had been, as I said, medical technology, at her parents' suggestion, rather than physical education, which was her first love as a born athlete. I was glad and supportive of this opportunity for her to pursue a career of her own choice. For over twenty years, she has grown and progressed as a successful librarian, highly respected and competent.

One time while I was counseling with a woman minister CPE student, she got on the subject of difference between her role and the higher status of her husband physician. I shared a description of the comparison between Kathie's and my professional competence and status. I said flat out, "Kathie is a

better Law Librarian than I am a Professor." She was startled
with compassion for my difficult situation, "That must be very
difficult for you." I replied, "What is so bad about being married
to a very competent and successful spouse? Would it be better if
she were some kind of failure, and I could then use that to make
me feel good about myself? It makes me feel more worthwhile
knowing that such a competent person is willing to be my
spouse." "I hadn't thought about it like that," she commented.
"Furthermore," I continued, "did you hear what I said? Is it
useful to state the issue in this way in the first place? At the
County Fair, do they compare apples and carrots, sheep with
chickens? Comparative adjectives must be used accurately and
appropriately." From then on she worked at accepting herself for
who she was and accepting her husband for what he was
according to competence, money, you name it. As Kathie entered
more fully into her professional role, I helped out around the
house, even occasionally cooking dinner in the wok pan. It was
fun, and I didn't even wait for the women's movement to tell me
it was the right and just thing to do. Once I recall wondering
how Kathie could go off to a law librarian convention in Chicago
or Los Angeles and stay in a big hotel with all kinds of strange
people roaming about. I quickly came to my senses and
remembered how many conventions, conferences and speaking
engagements had sent me out of town for a few days. Adjustment
to change doesn't come all at once. I would say the last twenty
years of our marriage have been constructively and stylistically
different from the first twenty. They were definitely two stages
in two different time frames.

Life has been so good for us in Iowa City that we plan to
retire here permanently, right here at 104 Sunset Street, where
we have lived since October, 1964. Considering how often my
folks moved after Barsness, and how often I changed addresses

before marriage, and the fact that, on average, an American family moves every four years, it has been a great satisfaction and feeling of security to have had this one home base for nearly thirty years.

It has been great fun to visit Kurt and Gretchen and the two cute grandchildren shown below. Twice a year is not enough to keep up on their rapid growth. Erik already swims up a storm, and just the other day Kate ducked her head under water. They keep us young and excited.

Here's the Family
August 1, 1992

Karl, Kit, Gretchen,
Kate, Kurt, Erik, Kathie, David

CHAPTER XIV

THE FARM

One of the attractive aspects of life in Iowa City was the happy reality that the open country was so close at hand. In only a few minutes we could be surrounded by cornfields and woods with creeks here and there. In the Twin Cities we had to pass through mile after mile of sprawling suburbs before reaching the wide open spaces.

It was not long after Kathie began working at the Law Library that she discovered that the parents of one of her co-workers owned a farm up by the Coralville Reservoir. Best of all, there were horses there for her and Kit to ride. With the possibility of buying these creatures, the next question arose. Could we find land of our own on which to pasture them?

Many Sunday afternoon tours of the environs finally turned up a delightful piece of land, forty acres, with plenty of trees for shade and the sizable Dirty Face Creek for the horses to drink their fill. We bought the land and three horses.

Transporting the beasts was our first challenge of horsewomanship. It turned out the herd consisted of a mature mare and her daughter and son, he less than a year old. A local call located a man with a pickup truck, who claimed to be a competent horse hauler. Sunday, April 8, 1973, began as an innocent enough day. He called and reported he had found a trailer and was undaunted by the late snow that was falling. By the time we reached the loading site, we wondered if this was an auspicious time to begin ranching. The sight of the small, flimsy, two-wheel trailer did nothing to reassure us. He claimed he could squeeze them in with a large shoehorn by wedging the little one backwards between the two adults. So we were ready to head south.

"We'll have to skirt around Iowa City since my turn signals do not work; and it will get dark soon," was his next contribution to our consternation. No sooner had we skittered around the city and rejoined Highway 218 than he developed a flat tire. There I was, rolling the wheel back several blocks to a gas station for tire repair. My next job was to find the trailer again through the increasing blizzard. By the time we got to our forty-acre spread, eight inches of snow made it difficult to tell the road from the ditch. Fortunately, his headlights held out till the confused critters were released into their new home (no barn, mind you, just home on the range).

The next morning, driven by guilt, we rushed out to erect a snow wall the horses could use as shelter. We packed buckets of snow into building blocks. In retrospect, this was maybe unnecessary since the creek banks were ten feet tall, and other winters we found the horses, and cows we had bought, hiding there for shelter even after we had built a small barn and left the door open. We would have much to learn.

We learned it was not necessary nor prudent to grub out stumps and logs from the creek to make it neater. An ecology pamphlet explained that these obstacles created eddies and whirlpools that hollowed out good habitat for fish and hiding places to protect them from predators.

It was also possible for us to create much work for ourselves when we finally got some cattle. I had a farmer place the large round bales of hay on a hill south of the creek to keep them nice and dry. The well and watering tank were on the north side of the creek. When the ten-foot-deep creekbed filled with snow to the brim, we decided to carve out a trench for the animals to cross from food to water and back to food again. We did not lack for exercise.

Speaking of cattle, I must relate how my herd of Black Angus originated. I confidently went to the Hills Bank and Trust to borrow enough to buy fifteen heifers at 48¢ a pound. They would drink free of charge from the creek and graze on the meadow as the Lord provided. By fall they would have doubled their weight, but, by then the price was 27¢ a pound. So I decided to buy hay and keep them over the winter until prices went up or their weight did. To my great shock a bull broke into our pasture and ravaged those innocent heifers who were entrusted in my paternal care. The neighbor farmer teased me thus: "Say, Dave, where did you cut the fence so the bull could get into your pasture?" I then realized that I had just saved considerable in breeding fees. By the third year I had sold enough to have left a mature herd of eight cows free and clear. The herd built up to twenty-three. The reason I gave up on cattle was because of the "baas" and "fishda" (remember the story of the Lantern Man and the poop pile by the door?). Well, let me assure you it was no joke when such a group deposited their feces all over the floor and then proceeded to cover same with a thin layer of urine, which froze into a small, brown mountain. Have you ever tried cleaning the barn with an ax in February? Don't even try it; just go back to golf for your hobby, or swimming in the Field House for exercise.

Let us turn our attention to plants, which tend to make less of a mess. We planted hundreds of evergreen trees in a part of the pasture we fenced out for conservation. One hundred-fifty survived and today are between thirty and forty feet tall. Also, oak and walnut trees volunteered; and other deciduous trees were planted by squirrels who forgot where they had hidden their prizes. Some seeds just fell off the mother tree and grew in clusters.

Later a buddy, Clayton Ringgenberg, and I planted about forty apple trees. One Delicious brand tree alone bore eight bushels last year. It was well worth the wait for them to mature enough to bear. A few weeks ago our wives and we pressed thirty gallons of apple cider. The farm was a great recreation.

Gardening was also a great sport for Kathie and me. In four gardens we raised nineteen kinds of fruits and vegetables. A year ago we had potatoes that lasted us until the following April. Kathie looked forward to harvesting enough strawberries and raspberries and grapes to make jelly and jam enough for the year.

My favorite psychologist, Gordon Allport, used the term "functional autonomy" to describe an activity or life-style which may have been necessary at one time being transformed into another purpose such as recreation. Remember my telling about growing popcorn to earn money for necessities? On this farm I was growing it for fun. Once I had a very early crop and stopped by my neighbor, Junior Maas, to give him a dozen ears of sweet corn long before his was ready. I teased him, "I hate to see the farmer's children go without sweet corn." Oh, yes, I could become competitive when I wanted to. When I served a Bloody Mary to the pre-football game crowd on our back deck, I always just happened to comment that they were made with my own tomato juice.

We mowed a large yard which served well for entertaining groups of friends and sometimes students from the CPE program at University Hospital. I built a brick fireplace. There was electricity in the 20 x 50 foot pole barn we had built. At the picnic end was a paneled tack room with a concrete floor, and at the other end was Johnson County's only indoor outhouse with its own swinging door and Sears port-a-potty. Folks were amazed at

the progressive title over the door, PERSONS' ROOM. The
biggest gathering was almost a hundred under two rented tents.

Proud of sweet corn
eight feet tall.

Good! An ecologist
said we didn't need to
clean up this mess.

The family had many a picnic at the farm, sometimes connected with recreational work like building fence or loading cattle into a lo-boy trailer for hauling to market. My own nervousness spooked the cattle, and we would have to round them up all over again. I was glad this farming was not my sole means of support. Kathie has always understood animals better than I did, and the kids thought it was all pretty hilarious. Could this also have been a repetition of my father's view--doing something useful as sufficient fun? Oh, there were also rollicking games (see photo of Karl taking on the Old Man in horseshoes).

Speaking of animals, remember our original reason for acquiring the land was to have a place to pasture and ride the horses? Kit and Kathie may be seen in the accompanying photo training Nosey. Kit is shown not even using a saddle. It was a great mother-daughter pastime. The little fellow, Rascal, never did take to training, turned into a delinquent and a dropout. He was dropped from the class when he kicked Kathie so hard on her thigh that it left a tattoo mark of his hoof for weeks. *Heraus mit dir!* So that left the mother riding the mother and the daughter riding the daughter. It was a joy to behold (from a distance).

I have come to wonder why gardening is not used more often as a test of personality and character. The overachiever could be quickly diagnosed, as in my case. In the spring I always had high hopes and plowed up one plot after another. I had forgotten completely the lesson from the previous year when I should have learned that it does not pay to bite off more of Mother Earth than you can chew (if that is not too cannibalistic a figure of speech). The rows of onions and squared-off hills of squash looked neat and orderly as they grew green and obedient. Then we would go off for a week or so on holiday; and when we returned our fears were realized. By then the weeds were taller than the crops. The garden had its mid-life crisis: to try to restore order at great cost of time and energy, or to let nature take its course. My thoughts often turned to the thirteenth chapter of Matthew.

> … an enemy came and sowed weeds among the wheat, and went away … Let both grow together until the harvest; and at harvest time I will tell the reapers, 'Gather the weeds first and bind them in bundles to be burned, but gather the wheat into my barn.'

This last fall I spread straw over the whole garden, put lighter fluid all over it, and set it aflame. This was to kill the crabgrass seeds so they would not come up next year. I did this after hunting for the onions, which had been smothered as thoroughly as if they had been planted among the bent grass of a putting green. Some years I got a good crop of one kind and not another. Alternate years something else would thrive and something else would drown in competitive greenery. Nothing has kept me more humble than those gardens.

Everything considered, The Farm was a great diversion for me and the family. The sedentary workers, especially academic types, really benefit by getting in touch with nature and reality once in a while. At least that is how it worked for me.

Karl shows his Dad
that horseshoes can be
serious business.

Mowing the weeds on
the meadow with my
forty-year-old 8-N
Ford tractor. Just
because it was
necessary did not
mean it wasn't fun.

The bad boy, Rascal, who kicked his mistress, I mean really hard!

Oh, yes, Kit used a saddle later on, but here, she and Nosey are just getting acquainted with each other.

CHAPTER XV

DEPARTURES AND TERMINATIONS

I've spoken at great length about my own family and our life together; but, of course, I have also been an integral member of my family origin. In the normal life cycle, as a person hits his/her stride in mid-life, losses begin to occur; the previous generation begins dying off. Not long after losing Grandpa or Grandma, you wake up one morning to realize that now you are the Grandpa; you have become the next patriarch. Such was my experience, in due time, since my parents died in old age. The three deaths in my family of origin are as follows:

Papa died in 1969 at age 88 when I was 47
Mama died in 1980 at age 92 when I was 58
Harold died in 1989 at age 77 when I was 67

The Psalmist admonished:

So teach us to number our days,
that we may apply our hearts unto wisdom.

The meaning of life comes into sharper focus when a loved one dies and we are reminded also of our own mortality. This is more true for me at my present age than when my maternal grandparents died toward the end of my adolescence.

In many ways I think Papa's life was more pleasant in retirement than at any other time in his life. At the time they lived in their last apartment in Minneapolis, a friendly neighbor let Papa plant two rows of sweet corn just west of his garage. Brother Harold wrote this positive statement in a memorial article:

A week before his death, at 88, he watched the Twins play baseball, read the daily news and studied Paul's letter to the Romans.

One day Papa fell in the bathroom, maybe from a stroke, and was taken to Deaconess Hospital in South Minneapolis. He was there only a very few days before he died. His family doctor, who was the son of another Norwegian Lutheran pastor, understood how inappropriate it would be to carry out any heroic measures; and so Papa died in peace with comfort care. The Greeks would have called it a "good death" *(eu-thanatos)*.

I am convinced that those old Norwegians of that generation faced and accepted death in a realistic and wholesome way, as the natural end of a long life cycle. When my maternal grandfather, Hans Johnshoy, was almost ninety, he harvested his garden seeds and put them in brown paper bags in his woodshed, each one labeled properly. He explained to me that was to provide for the eventuality that if he were not around next spring, someone else could continue gardening where he left off. I have also taken this view.

Although I naturally missed my father, I never sensed the kind of sorrow that comes with tragedy, which afflicts some who must contend with an "untimely death." He died in a state of grace, which means being in fellowship with your God and your family and your neighbor.

Mama's trajectory was longer; and gradually she became weaker over several years at Ebenezer Nursing Home. She received compassionate care, but was also blessed with a positive attitude and acceptance of her situation. She imitated Saint Paul, who wrote, "I have learned, in whatever state I am, to be content." I have found that people age and die as they have lived, whether as pessimists or optimists (excluding brain damage,

Alzheimer's disease, etc.). Also, Mama's generation somehow
had strong constitutions since they could keep on surviving when
they were as frail as a leaf ready to fall from the tree in late fall.
After all, they had survived the flu epidemic, diphtheria,
whooping cough, pneumonia, small pox, and what all when there
were no miracle drugs, which came on the market at the time of
World War II. Mama shriveled in size but not in disposition.
Even when she was so weak she could hardly speak, she would
smile; and her physician commented, "I believe she has a rich
interior life." That is when a pleasant, positive attitude pays off.
She also, like Papa, died in what the Bible calls "the fullness of
time" (an appropriate time).

The postlude for Mama's funeral was the hymn, "For all
the saints who from their labors rest." Yes, she deserved a rest
after all her laboring in the Kingdom and for her family. Papa's
postlude was a brass quartet's rendition of Handel's "The Trumpet
Shall Sound." That strong, no nonsense piece seemed to typify
Papa's life and faith. As I walked down the aisle it was as though
the music was escorting me out. I have chosen that postlude for
my final service and hope that George Paterson will play it on his
trombone (if he outlives me).

Harold's death was another matter. We siblings are
supposed to be together as a group, peers, all from the same
generation. This is coming closer to home. By then I was
retired, and Harold died at age seventy-seven. Harold's brand of
stoicism was to keep his cancer secret for several years. He
sickened at home and finally entered a nursing home. It was a
hard and lonesome journey for him.

Harold was a critic and a gadfly, championing the cause of
the poor and oppressed. Ever since his days at Luther College he
had been a nonconformist. This crystalized in his studies in
literary criticism at the University of Iowa. It is not unusual

among such scholars to doubt authorship and challenge established theories. Maybe someone else wrote this play generally and traditionally attributed to Shakespeare. In such circles the same was said about certain books of the Bible. Very likely other authors wrote parts of what were called the Five Books of Moses, the Pentateuch. There was also a Second Isaiah and on and on. You can imagine what arguments were generated when he brought these new ideas to Papa's attention. Harold tended to be quite dogmatic once he entered a fray whether the topic was Scripture, politics, economics, social welfare or church politics. He was a scrapper. Even after his retirement he continued to conduct seminars and conferences comparing the social ethics of Karl Marx and Jesus, usually with an antiestablishment bent.

I felt two ways about Harold's reformist mission. First, I was challenged and sensitized to issues of justice and the radical implications of the social ethics of prophets such as Amos and Micah and, of course, Jesus, for our own time. Secondly, I was sometimes embarrassed by his abrasiveness and singlemindedness. Ever since my university days I have been uncomfortable with the fundamentalist hyper-certainty of a person whether it be in matters of religion, politics, or economics. No matter where Harold met a conservative or a Republican, whether in business, professional or social circles, an argument would begin quickly and continue along predictable channels until a wide gap of polarization was created and the discussion got nowhere.

We all have our hang-ups but, underneath, I had a deep brotherly affection and regard for Harold. I took this loss harder than I thought I would. The Sunday after his funeral, I was conducting a service in a Lutheran church; and during the Benediction I broke down and could not finish it. This surprised me because I had always thought of myself as very much in control of myself in public speaking events. Something else

happened at the funeral with which I did not agree. I was asked
to read a poem from Robert Frost, which Harold had requested
for the service. Sometimes it happens that a son, brother or sister
is asked to take a leadership role when the person would be better
off taking the mourner role, i.e., being ministered unto. He or
she might be better off just sitting in a pew and grieving, or
receiving as needed, instead of putting on a brave front and being
complimented for "holding up so well" under the circumstances.

At any rate, Papa, Mama, and Harold have departed; and
Joe, Dorothy and I remain at the time of this writing.

Terminations

Beyond these very personal, familial encounters with
separation, grief and bereavement, I have also dealt with death
and loss professionally as a pastor and chaplain, and, also, as an
academic study in courses and seminars I have taught.

Routinely, in Clinical Pastoral Education, we wrestled with
how to terminate an interview with a patient in the hospital or in
a counseling situation. I maintained that the counselor was
responsible for structuring the beginning of the session and for
bringing it to a close. Meanwhile, the time and content and use of
the intervening period was largely up to the client or patient (e.g.,
what to talk about, how deeply to delve into an issue, etc.). I
learned early in my ministry that in the case of a lonely person,
my goal could not be "to meet his/her needs." What the person
really needed was to have someone with whom to eat breakfast,
lunch and dinner. I had to decide what my role and task were and
then terminate at a fitting time, not hope that terminating would
somehow take care of itself. Students found this difficult since
sometimes their own needs got mixed into the equation, and it felt
so good to be needed that they did not want to terminate either a

session or a series of sessions. When a patient would leave University Hospital to return to Sioux City, way across the state, the student-chaplain might say a kind of *Auf wieder sehen* or some other equivalent of "See you around" rather than a straightforward "Good-bye."

The pastor of First Presbyterian Church in Iowa City was retiring after twenty-six years of service. He told me, "You know, Dave, I know a minister should not stay around and stick his nose into his successor's business; and I know myself well enough to know that I would--so we're moving to Arizona." He was making it crystal clear that he had terminated his role as pastor of that church and was moving on to other things.

Termination by death is not the only kind of separation that can be painful. It was not easy for Kathie to leave her friends and choir in Minneapolis. Some family might delay making a vocational move until the youngest has finished high school.

Retirement can be traumatic as one loses a "place in society" and familiar setting and faces. For me, retirement was very clear-cut and satisfying, a task concluded, mission accomplished. I felt good about handing my role over to my successor.

It remains to be seen if I will have equal equanimity about the end of my own life whenever that time comes. In the numerous funerals I have conducted, our tradition has this statement, said at the grave just before sprinkling earth on the casket three times:

> In the midst of life we are in death.
> Of whom may we seek for succor but of thee, O Lord ...
> O holy and most merciful Saviour:
> Suffer us not, at our last hour
> for any pains of death, to fall from thee.

I never tire of this passage and always find it meaningful and helpful.

Now that I have spoken about leaving and separating, I suppose you wonder what became of me when I left the University and my retirement was signified by a new title: Emeritus. I'll tell you about it later on.

CHAPTER XVI

RUNNING HEADLONG INTO POLITICS

> You might well ask, "How could a law-abiding citizen, a Norwegian Lutheran pastor, faithfully serving as a professor of religion in a state university: indeed!--how *could* such a one become Iowa's only Socialist mayor?" But there I was, minding my own business, cutting out dandelions from my lawn and trimming my hedge like a standard suburbanite one bright fall day; and the next thing I knew, I was Mayor of University Heights--thereafter to be addressed as His Honor, the Reverend Professor. It was too much.

(Taken from a little paperback I published myself for fun, satire and challenge, entitled *Memoirs of Iowa's Only Socialist Mayor*, 1990, about being University Heights Mayor, 1970-1976.)

As in the case of most small towns of 1,200, serving as town councilperson or mayor is no big deal, and the $50 per month stipend is not usually what rescues such volunteers from the poverty level. It is more or less like passing around certain committee assignments in a faculty or at any other club. So it was with me, a chance to learn about a function of our society I had never given any thought to before. In retrospect I wonder if Papa would have benefited by such an internship to prepare more fully for church politics. After all, CPE had not been invented then. It took me six years, three terms, to finish the course.

Newspapers, always desperate for enough news to fill the space not used for advertising, seize upon tidbits such as "Alice Jones, retired school teacher, runs for School Board." An innocent enough looking fellow in the front row of my Religion and Personality class held up his hand to ask a question, which I permitted. "Don't you think that a clergyman serving as mayor would be violating the well established principle of 'separation of church and state'?" (assuming that becoming ordained meant you

relinquished your citizenship in the Kingdom of This World).
Since I never knew when to be serious and when to have fun, this
student (I did not know he was a cub reporter for the *Daily
Iowan,* a laboratory for the School of Journalism), ran this item
the next morning:

**MAYOR BELGUM
GETS NEW FLOCK**

**Dr. David Belgum, religion professor and
Lutheran minister, gave this comment
during a class lecture concerning his recent
election as Mayor of University Heights:**

**"I don't feel it is violating the separation
of church and State at all . . . it's just the
largest congregation that I've ever had!"**

I relished the opportunity to teach our community and
others interested about the nature of our society (from the Latin
word <u>socius,</u> which means comrade or companion and from
which sociable and socialism are also derived). I pointed out that
the largest metal sculpture or artistic structure in most every
small town in Iowa is a symbol of socialism. It is the community-
owned water tower, and rich and poor drink out of the same
fountain at the park or schoolhouse. The same may be said of the
municipal sewage plant, but we need not go into that.

Some archaic terminology from a former life-style, more
individualistic and property oriented, still lingers on in our Town
Council meetings when it comes to assessing funds to pay for
street improvements. A home owner pays the levy because
"benefit is conferred upon that property." Literally, I suppose no
one else should drive on the street thus benefiting the property
owner's land. Yet the said person has the full right to drive back
and forth on that piece of concrete for which he has paid. Almost

the only way to get to work or school would be to trespass on someone else's concrete. It is hard to be consistent in our social and political philosophy. Many of these discussions broke down before they even got started. It was not the easiest course to teach.

So many, like the reporter in my class, assume religion and politics should not mix. I found it difficult to be that purist. A couple weeks before the election I was invited to preach at the Saint Andrew Presbyterian Church across the street from our house. What should I choose for a text? I thought, naturally , the budget of the town, because it is there one finds the moral and ethical commitments of the citizens of a given area. It is not what people say they believe, it is what they are willing to pay for, in this case taxes. They were right on target according to the Hebrew Bible because they all agreed to "cast all unclean things outside the city wall." So they all agreed to pay to have such matter hauled to a landfill. We could go on and on, but you get the point.

I tried not to be preachy, but sometimes it may have sounded that way. I cite the following case and ask you to be the judge of whether I had overstepped my bounds:

> During one heated public hearing concerning the construction of sidewalks, various arguments for and against were presented. The "Friends of Little Children" wanted a safer walkway for their little ones as they wandered to the elementary school and reasoned that separating the school buses, cars and other vehicular traffic from pedestrian traffic would tend toward safety. Without sidewalks kids follow the path of least resistance and walk in the street. The "Defenders of Private Property" group claimed that they had moved to our town precisely because it did not have sidewalks but long stretches of grass uninterrupted by slabs of citified concrete between house and curb.

A person of known, above average income (since all salaries of
faculty staff in the university are published annually in the *Des
Moines Register)* rose to make a telling point. The family had
been planning a trip to England the following summer. With
tremulous voice the question was posed: "What will that do to
my vacation?" Knowing the person's keen interest in antiques
and trying to be helpful, I quickly calculated in my head how
they could accommodate the $367.00 sidewalk improvement
assessment and still make ends meet. I ventured the following
unsolicited advice: "You might consider buying one fewer
antique Wedgewood cream pitcher." I have no way of knowing
whether this advice was helpful, but the sidewalk issue was
settled later that evening in favor of construction. Now the
citizens on that street say, when I ask them how they like the
new sidewalk, "What new sidewalk? Wasn't it always here?"

On the one hand I saw my role as the benevolent dictator
doing what was good for the masses. For example, I proposed
(and it passed the council) that we plow snow from all sidewalks
in the entire town since many of our elderly and handicapped
could not do this chore and could not find young boys who would
stoop so low as to do it either. Before long there were irate
complaints that the snow plow had chipped or cracked some
sidewalk, etc. Then one morning toward the end of winter there
was a warm spell. The ground thawed and snow fell upon the
soft earth. I was horror-struck to realize that the tractor might
leave a ditch on either side of the sidewalk and we would have to
re-sod for several miles. I hastily called off the snow plower just
in time, and we returned to the more conservative, individualistic,
each-one-take-care-of-him/herself way; actually more typical of
the ethos in Iowa.

At the other extreme I could be very understanding and
empathetic with citizens at public hearings. Not enough has been
made of the psychotherapeutic aspects of public administration.
There was hardly a pastoral care problem in my Danish Lutheran
parish in the slum section of Boston which was not replicated in

my career as mayor of this nice suburb, including one wedding and two funerals, much counseling, group therapy, home visitation, and a certain amount of Ladies Aid work, to say nothing of informal arbitration of over-the-back-fence neighborhood disputes. Some of the warmest compliments I received during my three terms as mayor came after I had conducted an unusually knotty open hearing on some public works project--statements to the effect that the session had been "helpful" and "therapeutic."

I felt I had served and learned enough during these six years. I found it all very interesting, but it would be only fair to pass on the torch to some neighbor who could also benefit and grow through this experience. Thus ended the socialist reign over University Heights, 1970-1976. Things went back to normal after that.

In another decade I was sure that if I stood on a kitchen chair I would be able to see retirement on the horizon. I thought that after twenty-three years of building up the Department of Pastoral Services, I had maybe used up any good ideas I had. Time to hand over the reigns to someone else. I had gotten a plaque from the College of Chaplains indicating I had rendered "Distinguished Service" and "Outstanding contributions to hospital chaplaincy, clinical pastoral education and the relationship between faith and health." Also, I was awarded a certificate of "Distinguished Independent Study Course" for my correspondence course, Death and Dying, by the National University Continuing Education Association. As Mama would have said, "They sure have been good to you, David." It had been a good career, and I was satisfied.

But I still had good health and a relatively alert mind. Now that my career in academe was over, what should I do with myself? I set my cap for even loftier heights in politics. I would

run for the office of Supervisor of Johnson County. Imagine my
going from a congregation of 1,200 souls to 80,000; for being
responsible for between 3 and 4 miles of street to caring for 923
miles of road crossing 272 bridges 20 feet or more in length.
Was I overreaching myself? Only the voters would know and
decide. I decided to campaign the way I knew best, by making as
many pastoral calls on as many of these prospective parishioners
as possible.

In Oxford I sat down with a couple ruggedly dressed men
in a bar to give them my brochure and enter into conversation.
One of my pet projects to beautify the countryside and make it
look less run-down at the heels was to have youth groups, like the
4-H or Future Farmers of America, gather up old scrap metal and
bring it to certain intersections where a semi would be loaded.
The proceeds could be divided between the farmer whose metal it
was and the group collecting it. Everyone would benefit. I was
determined to make this a positive statement and speak of "re-
usable metal" or "salvageable parts," surely not junk. I got my
comeuppance.

"Aw Hell!" the less shaven one whistled through his missing
tooth, "that's what my wife says. Claims I should get rid of those
three old cars between the back porch and her blame garden."

"Maybe they'd bring some money from a salvage yard," I
ventured.

"You don't understand nothin," was his tender retort. "The
other day I needed a radiator for my pick-up. I tore the radiator
out of my old Dodge Dart; and Geez the old fart was as good as
new--still had the anti-freeze in it. Where'd I be if I'd got rid of
that son-uva-bitch--hadta bought a new one, that's what."

He took a glance at my Hawkeye colored black and gold
brochure, a color combination unashamedly intended to win over
the large football fan contingent.

"Says here you usta be a university perfessor ... That figgers." Clearly I was not going to win a convert, so I pressed on, looking for greener pastures. Pancake breakfasts were a must on the campaign trail. I shook hundreds of hands at eight such events. Once I licked enough maple syrup off my fingers as a result of handshaking to make a whole meal. With coffee in left hand and brochures under left elbow, it was still possible to extend a sincere right hand and sometimes get it shaken. This table hopping was duck soup for me since I had been well trained at church suppers to do this very thing, only then the brochures would be about missions, world relief, etc.

One Sunday down by Lone Tree, I left the American Legion Hall pancake breakfast to strike out into the countryside and make my round of farms. The first place was inhabited by a retired couple. The lady of the house was so pleased that a person of my qualifications would be willing to serve the public as Supervisor. "We need more people like you in politics. By the way, I got so much out of your course when it was broadcast over the university station. Lots of luck. We're all for you; aren't we Al?" Al nodded obediently. That kind of ego boost sent me fairly floating down the gravel road in my new black Ford pick-up truck. At the next place I thought for sure I was seeing my Norwegian farmer uncle striding in a deliberate way between the hog house and the cow barn. I pulled up by him and stopped. Hoping he would keep the rather large-mouthed dog under control, I attempted to alight from the truck with a certain air of macho self-confidence. I held the brochure between me and the dog. He could chew on that while I scrambled back into the truck and lost another vote.

"Ya, I know who you are! If there's anything we don't need, it's a retired university professor on the Board of Supervisors." He turned his attention away from me and any

speech I might have been prepared to make and toward the hogs
who, he felt, needed his attention more. Maybe he was right;
after all, I'd just eaten and the hogs hadn't evidently.

Misjudging a Power Base

I was not so naive to think a candidate did not need a
constituency, a power base. I suppose I had preached in almost
half the churches in the county (as many of us on the faculty who
happened to be ordained had been invited to do on a fill-in basis).
I had even spoken from the pulpit of Saint Thomas More and
spoken at the local synagogue. And there were many other
speaking engagements on an assortment of topics, which people
had been kind enough to say were helpful. I counted on that,
name recognition and all. It became clear to me that there was
another way to build a power base if one wants to be elected as a
County Supervisor. First, be President of the Shorthorn
Cattleman's Association and then President of the Farm Bureau's
local chapter. Finally, it helps if you volunteer to sell football and
basketball tickets to the Irish Catholic Democrats at Regina High
School. My opponent did all these things and won handily.

So what if our little forty-acre spread and one-time twenty-
three head herd of Black Angus did not ingratiate me with the
farmers and make me appear to be one of them; at least I had the
laborers on my side--after all, they had nothing to lose but their
chains. I had always considered myself a member of the
proletariat. Had I not written books for approximately $1.47 an
hour before taxes and many learned articles for no recompense
whatsoever? When one calculates preparation time and car
expense going to and from the pulpit site, actually delivering the
sermon, etc., my compensation often came to well below

minimum wage. Surely I was a friend of labor if not one of them.

As it turned out hardly any laborers had read any of my books to say nothing of my journal articles. Worse yet, they had not heard my sermons. None of them knew I had been Iowa's only Socialist mayor. So be it; we all had an equal opportunity to appear before the laborers of the county at a union hall. After sufficient beer to get the meeting under way plus the usual chitchat, we candidates were invited to sit at the head folding table. We all fielded the questions as best we could and departed while the Union Council made up their mind whom to endorse as their favorite. It was not I. Evidently they saw through my hypocrisy like one can see through a very old dishrag.

Some knowledgeable politicos counseled me that it would take a lot to overcome the stigma of having worked in academe for twenty-three years. I had assumed that working for the largest socialist institution in the state (a state-owned and state-run university) would have endeared me to the masses who paid taxes for its support.

Another class with whom I failed can be best epitomized by a small coterie gathered around common values and life-style, the habitués of a certain rural garage. I had been told by a knowledgeable supporter of my campaign that a whistle stop at this site was essential for winning that entire township. When I arrived, I found a group of nine persons standing about while the master of ceremonies, who handled his wrench like a gavel, presided over the discussion. The meeting was held in a three-bay garage behind the gas station office. Some sat on packing crates or on a low stack of tires, others leaned against the wall, door frame or Coke machine. Most drank beer or Coke. A timid looking fellow, in striped railroad worker coveralls, sipped self-consciously on a quart carton of chocolate milk. My long interest in linguistics soon made me focus more on their discourse and vocabulary than my own reason for being there. After distributing my brochure, I mostly listened to their colorful and symbolic language. A literal translation follows:

"Oh (Hades)! This (condemned by God) carburetor ain't worth the (defecation) it's made of," said the self-assertive owner-mechanic.

"If you ask me, those (male descendants of female dogs) in Detroit can't tell their (anus) from a hole in the ground," was said by next in line. "They just don't give a (sexual intercourse) about quality."

Number three was now up to bat. "Oh (second Person of the Trinity)! I'm (urinated) about the whole (sexual intercourse) (Condemned by God) (Male descendants of female dogs) mess."

Now it was time for our chocolate-slurping youngest member of the team to be at bat. All eyes and ears were alert. Could he; would he make it? He stepped up and spat a piece from the carton out of the corner of his mouth. He turned to the membership chairman of the fraternity for guidance; but he was on his own. He took a deep breath.

"Aw shucks," he began in a low voice with both fists firmly embedded in his coverall pockets, "Ya gotta expect trouble every now and then. Heck, Jack; you'll be able to fix the darn thing."

The other members of the club looked down sheepishly. He had clearly not passed muster, and would need to mature some more before he was eligible. They also looked somewhat accusingly at me, which I understood meant that they suspected my presence had intimidated the candidate. Perhaps some of them had heard that I had preached a few times at Sharon Center United Methodist Church only a few miles south over the ridge. I did not even ask them for contributions to my campaign.

It takes a lot of self-confidence to be a good beggar. I should not have felt intimidated by the stigma of asking for a handout; after all Martin Luther began his career as a begging monk. To me it dredged up memories of the Great Depression; and I have never found poverty that character building. Was I really entitled to go up to an old friend and say, "If you will give me some of your hard-earned cash, I will get a cushy political plum and be supported by taxpayers like yourself"? One of my affluent relatives in the world of private business once asked me concerning my job at the University, "Dave, are you still slopping at the public trough?"

I knew full well that every penny would have to be accounted for. In my packet of materials from the County Auditor and Commissioner of Elections, there were heavy phrases such as "Disclosure Summary," "Please Complete All Blanks," and "See Manual for Compliance." How much simpler it was to run for mayor of University Heights. On this same type of form sent me a dozen years before from the state capitol, I had honestly reported that my total expense for the entire campaign for Mayor was the cost of the postage stamp to return that very form. At the County level, my expenses ran into the dozens, even hundreds of dollars. Nevertheless, I cannot honestly say that more money would have made the difference between defeat and victory.

One of the wealthiest persons I approached, from whom I expected a large handout for old times' sake, replied apologetically, "I'd love to help you out Dave, but ______ (one of my opponents) and I go back a long way. You see, I played the role of his father in our high school class play." Guess I was the new kid on the block.

And what does it feel like when you lose such an election and your friends and neighbors have invested in you? From that experience I knew what the failed S&L managers must go through.

Oh yes, I could easily have gone over my head and reached the level of my incompetence. Some may call this rationalization; actually it is Norwegian common sense. If it is worded properly, one can even get credit for humility. So where should I go from here, now that I have received continuing education credits in political science and a fascinating opportunity to tour the county?

Before I tell you what became of me next, I want to share what other continuing education experiences I had partly due to my having been involved in academe and partly by my own design and good luck.

CHAPTER XVII

TRAVEL AS CONTINUING EDUCATION

How does one keep from getting into a rut in academe, teaching the same classes, going to the same staff meetings, and on and on? I say, "By getting away from it all." One gains perspective from drawing away from the daily scene and then returning and seeing everything new again. I did not start out to be a traveler, but turned out to be one. When I was a kid it was a great trip to go the five miles to Glenwood and later ten miles to the county fair.

My first significant journey came about with the good excuse of attending the Lutheran World Federation meeting in Helsinki, Finland, in the summer of 1963. Not that I was a delegate or anything special. There was just a very reasonably priced tour package for Lutheran pastors, which included England and a quick tour down as far as Switzerland. Literally a high point was the cable car ride to the top of Mount Pilatus. We went swinging up to 7,000 feet, but not without a fright for yours truly. About 2,000 feet up there was what seemed to me a tremendous jerk and loud click. I was sure we had run into a true emergency; but it was just passing over a very tall tower after which we seemed to descend a bit, but were just climbing another loop in time to click over another tower on the mountain side. It was so windy that this was the last ride up. At the top were breathtaking vistas in all four directions toward one famous peak after another. The clouds closed in, and the only way down was the cog railroad, which you can see crawling through and down the mountain at an amazing angle. It was actually a great relief to get down to the bottom where we caught a boat back to Lucerne.

You don't forget adventures like that. It almost seems unreal to get back to the pastoral scenes of Iowa.

History abounds. Part of the city wall and an old covered bridge both go back to the middle of the fourteenth century. In our town if a building is over fifty years old it can go on the Historic Register. I recall bragging to a fellow Boston University student from India that Boston went way back to 1620. He patiently told me his town was 4,000 years old. Oh, I see.

A dozen years later Kathie and I were to visit Kit over Easter when she was attending Freiburg University. That time my side objective was to visit, and take pictures of, the place where Jung had lived. He once said he always had to live by water. Sure enough, I found his birthplace on Lake Constance in the little village of Kesswil; then we went to where he spent a significant part of his childhood high above the Rhine Falls at the Laufen parsonage. I talked to the local pastor. It was from Pastor Jung's early departure from that charge that I got the idea of checking the minutes of my father's congregation. Pastor Jung was also an intellectual and a linguist and seemed not to have enjoyed the ministry. Finally, back on Lake Zurich, I not only saw Carl Gustav's famous home on the lake and visited with his son, Franz, who then lived there, but I also visited his important retreat at Bollingen further down the lake. It added a personal touch to the seminar and increased my interest in the topic. From that I decided to add a biographical essay about Jung to my textbook as a kind of model or sample of how to write the term paper I required analyzing a person's case history.

While the tour group did London in the 1963 trip, I ran up to Oxford to see what a really old university was like. So there I was where C. S. Lewis wrote his wonderful books that have inspired so many people puzzled about meaning in their lives once they had let go of religion. It stretched my mind.

The sabbatical in 1976 was a banner experience. First, I had gotten a routine announcement requesting papers for the First

International Congress on Seerat in Pakistan. I threw my hat into the ring with a topic, "Medical Ethics from the Perspective of Islam." It was a growing experience writing the paper but an even more remarkable experience delivering it in Karachi, Pakistan. It was a sizable and representative symposium with the Mufti of Turkey, the Imam of Mecca, dignitaries from every Middle East country and a few from Europe and North America. It was co-sponsored by the very wealthy Hamdard Foundation and its President, Hakim Mohammed Said, who made his fortune promoting Tibbi Medicine (especially the herbal and homeopathic approach); and also by the Minister of Religious Affairs. Remember, Islam has been the state religion of Pakistan ever since its separation from India. It would be equivalent to our President having a Secretary of Religion on his Cabinet.

Out of courtesy for the majority who were from Middle East and Arabic speaking countries, I sought out a graduate student at Lahore University who was willing to translate my talk into the Arabic language. Then I had enough copies printed so it could be available to all who wished it. They seemed to appreciate it. It was the least I could do in exchange for free board, room and hospitality for the two-week stay that the conference met. Our entire entourage went by bus to various sites with a few lectures being given at each place: Karachi, the largest city, ancient Lahore, Islamabad, the new capital, and Peshawar in the Northwest Territory near the Khyber Pass, which leads into Afghanistan.

I must say a few words about this last stop. It was unreal. First, just before our tour group approached the Pass with its customs house, we were entertained at a fabulous banquet in the home of a known smuggler. He owned a large fleet of trucks, which would unload their goods, place the contraband on camels, which walked around the checkpoint, and then the stuff was reloaded on trucks again. No government has ever succeeded in taming this region. Even Alexander the Great from Ancient Greece failed to take this territory, and the British were smart enough to leave it alone. The local chieftains administer their own rules and code of ethics, settle disputes and punish criminals. Meanwhile, at this feast a peasant came with a goat as an offering to the Imam of Mecca (equivalent to the Pope in Rome). The Imam laid his hands on the animal and returned it to the peasant. Obeisance observed!

At Islamabad the Speaker of the National Assembly was our host for lunch at the Islamabad Club. Hospitality throughout the stay was extraordinary. After lunch I walked in the vicinity and fell into conversation with a nice man who invited me into his home for a drink. Why not? We chatted amiably. He had been a high officer in the Pakistan Army before Bhutto came to power. It shook me up a bit, after I got home, to find that Bhutto had been executed in a coup. Maybe this nice general got his old job back; I don't know. I was obviously naive in my assessment of what it meant that there were army personnel in the corridors of our International Hotel at each stop. I thought, "My, what respect and honor our group is receiving." Actually, they were there in case of trouble against any of several dignitaries from rival countries.

I went with a newly formed acquaintance into the crowded bazaar of old Lahore. In one little shop I bought a beautiful wooden tray with inlaid copper cut into the wood in the shape of a flower and other designs. Then I wanted to buy Kathie a dress and was about to pay for it when my companion, more wise in Arabic customs than I, pulled me aside. "You can't just pay for it. You have to bargain and haggle over the price. Anything less is just not good etiquette." Well, I quickly saw I should turn over the bargaining to him. It came down in price so rapidly it made my head spin. The merchant was happy as a clam; and I was covered with Norwegian guilt.

We were taken on a visit into the controversial Kashmir District to see the Mangla Dam, the world's largest and longest earthen dam. There again was the gourmet lunch.

All invitations to receptions, dinners, etc., were on embossed cards with bumpy printing, which has always impressed me. The velvet-like red on embossed gold-colored card stock, shown below, contained the invitation to the dinner sponsored by the Writers Forum that was held at the Secretariat Ministry of Religious Affairs. I also got to attend a wedding. But the masses who showed up at the giant mosques were the most impressive of all--ten thousand or so bowing in prayer in unison at prescribed hours.

WRITERS FORUM

Visiting the 2,000-bed hospital in Karachi, I was struck by the contrast in health care between our societies. I made rounds with an Internal Medicine team who were trying to read an X-ray to see whether the patient had TB or pneumonia. A Bunsen burner sterilized instruments while cats licked the spilled milk off the floor. Patients' relatives had to bring in food for their family member. So how was America helping them with new technology? Still in its plastic wrapper and shipping crate, set to one side, was a brand spanking new hemodialysis machine. Obviously they did not have staff trained to run such a gadget; and if they did, they would rather allocate the staff time to get at basics before turning to exotics. The medical ethics principle that came into play here would be "the greatest good for the greatest number."

The year, 1976, had another great experience in store for me. I had taken an interest in the new group called US-China Peoples Friendship Association. It was one of several people-to-people efforts aimed at bridging the gap between societies and different cultures. I jumped at the chance to go on one of their early tours. In fact, we arrived only a month after Chairman Mao died and were there during the overthrow of the "Gang of Four" (including Mao's conniving widow). Since I had begun teaching a course on medical ethics, I was most interested in their health care delivery system, and naturally, published an article on "Medicine, Morals and Mao" in the *Journal of Religion and Health* upon my return home.

The universality of the Barefoot Doctor with his six months of first-aid-type training meant that everyone's health was checked into at a very elemental level. That is, there was a universal entry channel to the health care system--referrals being made to the equivalent of our county hospitals and then on to more specialized larger hospitals, like our university hospitals.

They dealt with venereal disease from a social perspective, e.g., why do women enter prostitution? We <u>call</u> it a <u>social</u> disease, but deal with it mostly in a scientific and technical manner or even a legal approach. They made drastic reductions in venereal disease; we have not. Their approach to the parasite problem of schistosomiasis was communal. Drain all the irrigation ditches (enormous hand labor project) and get rid of the snails that are the hosts of the parasite. They made great strides in reducing the disease. Oh, sure, I knew we were getting propaganda, just like I was shown the nice side of the slum of Roxbury by my good Danish hosts. This happens all the time. Nevertheless, it shakes one up to have to look at the world through the eyes of people so totally different in worldview and perspective from your own. I was a long way from Barsness or Chippewa Falls Lutheran Church, even a long way from Dr. Witts of Glenwood. It even seemed strange and new coming back to the University of Iowa Hospitals and Clinics with all its technological power and yet in the midst of a system leaving a very large minority uncovered by health insurance and falling to seventeenth place in infant mortality.

Kathie had also become enthusiastic about distant travel, and we had some great trips: Tanzania, where she managed to climb to the top of Mount Kilimanjaro (almost 20,000 feet), New Zealand, where she drove on the wrong side of the road from one end almost to the other, and Alaska.

The African safari was sponsored by the Iowa Mountaineers Club. I got to 15,000 feet before the altitude got to me and I had to stop at Kibo Hut, with a few other wimps, until the rest of the group returned the next afternoon. We saw native churches and mission efforts, health facilities, and village markets. Then it was off to the high plains, the Serengeti Desert,

isolated lodges and unbelievable scenes of nature and exotic
animals.

    After our New Zealand vacation, I stayed on for further
study, which I wrote up in an unpublished article, "Thoughts on
Health Care While in New Zealand." There I observed how an
entire health care system can be reversed if the opposition
political power gets into office. Nothing is permanent. I guess I
had thought once a great government sets something in place, it
remains forever like the Egyptian pyramids. Things change so
rapidly that even now, a large urban (or rural) renewal project
could easily remove a few pyramids from Main Street.

    When Kathie returned to her library job, I pressed on to
Papua New Guinea to see what health care might be like in a
primitive though developing country. They had had their own
parliament for about ten years, so the imprint of traditional

culture was very visible especially in the highlands where I went. A stay at the Melanesian Institute gave me good orientation. I learned from observation and talking with natives about the former head-hunting (now illegal), and sorcery, a deadly game. Westerners are now trying to figure out what makes many traditional remedies work: treatments made of roots, bark, berries, leaves, etc., which offer relief for diarrhea, headache, etc. I met a Ph.D. from Indiana who worked in such a research laboratory; and again, I had a chance to visit hospitals and clinics.

While a guest at Martin Luther Seminary at Lea, I was treated to hospitality by Kasek Kautil, who had studied in our CPE program at University Hospital in Iowa City. Together with lectures I was invited to give at the seminary and an invitation to preach in the capital city of Port Moresby for the pastor who came down with malaria, I spoke on seventeen occasions. Yet I was constantly learning more than I was giving, that's for sure. Kasek also arranged for a seminarian to take me for the weekend to his native village, a peaceful place forty miles from any road. We took a mail boat to a landing a mile from his village and walked the last stretch along the beach. Most harried American business types would pay a great deal of money to live in such a peaceful and quiet setting between the jungle and the sea for two weeks. At one intense community meeting to discuss who was the father of the child of an unmarried woman, the Lutheran Bishop was presiding. After the meeting adjourned about 11:30 Saturday night, he turned to me and said, "You preach tomorrow morning!" So, of course, I did. When in Rome, do as the Romans tell you--or something to that effect. Again, travel provided me with continuing education I never could have acquired back home, with or without academic credit. Oh, the article? Yes, but as yet unpublished except as I photocopied it and sent it to my former graduate students, "Learning About Health Care in Papua New Guinea."

A bonus that comes with writing articles and publishing books is that people get interested in your approach and ask you to come and address their group, convention or conference. This is common for university professors in all fields; and I am happy to say it was also so in my case. Along the way, continuing education took place as the discussion waxed pointed or side trips were educational.

For example, I may never have visited Banff in the national park west of Calgary, Alberta, if it had not been for speaking to the clergy in Moose Jaw and the large hospital in Calgary. One of the conference participants was a missionary to an Indian reservation, who kindly invited me to visit his mission site and then took me up to the Banff National Park. Such overnight hospitality was much appreciated.

The interdisciplinary field of religion-medicine was in vogue so I received invitations to conferences where both clergy and physicians were joined in discussion. Such was the case in Oklahoma City where the state medical association and the state council of churches had a joint conference. The same was true for Albuquerque, New Mexico, and the New York Mental Health Department (upstate). As a matter of fact, the reason professors are supposed to publish their ideas is precisely to expose them to public discussion. The writer/speaker constantly learns by feedback and discussion, criticism and sharpening of focus--more continuing education.

Two trips to Iceland were especially pleasant and stimulating. When the University of Iowa and Haskoli Islands (University of Iceland) became joined as sister institutions, the call went out for anyone wishing to go on an exchange lectureship for a short or long time. Like the little boy, Samuel, I held up

my hand and said, "Here am I, Lord, send me." And they did.
Since the Lutheran Church is the state church of Iceland, the
theological faculty (plus students) to whom I spoke were housed
right in the midst of the Administration Building. Then I also
spoke at the City Hospital and what we would consider the
University Hospital (national). The fact that I was invited back I
managed to have look like a compliment, to myself at least. A
side speaking trip to the north coast city of Akureyri, where I
spoke to local clergy and physicians, also generated a friendship
with the local pastor, Palmi Mattiasson. It was there that I
learned to go directly from an extremely hot hot tub directly into
rolling in the snow, then back into the hot tub only to walk across
ice to get back into the bath house. The next day I hoped I could
make it across the Arctic Circle by taking the mail plane to the
tiny island of Grimsey where rumor has it the Arctic Circle runs
right through the Pastor's parsonage bedroom. The wife sleeps
on one side of that line and the Pastor on the other. Be that as it
may, the one day I was free the weather was prohibitive.

At the time of the second trip, Pastor Palmi was serving in
the capital, Reykjavik. He knew how much I wanted to go out
into the North Sea on a fishing boat and arranged it. The captain
generously sent fifty pounds of cod and haddock home with me so
that Kathie and I could put on a fish supper for my parish when I
returned (more about this parish later).

Now, while the ink is drying on these pages, I have
returned from a lecture trip to Ireland where I spoke at the
invitation of Father Brendan Clifford, a Dominican monk who
was also a student in our CPE program at the University of Iowa
Hospital. By now you will be wondering if I went into teaching
knowing in advance I was going to have this much fun.
Nonsense, I was motivated totally by a desire to render Christian
service to those in need (Oh, excuse me; there I go again

mentioning Christian service through a state-owned university).
My assignments in Ireland included speaking to citizens of a
community which feels stigmatized by its poor reputation, a
group of the Dominican Order, clergy and physicians; and to top
it off, Brendan arranged for me to preach to a tiny Lutheran
church in Dublin on Sunday. Lutherans are even more scarce in
Dublin than in Boston as I found out.

Pastoral Therapy for Sick Parishes

Occasionally, about six or seven times, our Bishop in Iowa
called upon me to calm the troubled waters of a congregation
which had come through a ministerial maelstrom. There would
be a fuss of some kind: Tempest in a theological teapot,
disappointment over dreadful decisions, impropriety in pastoral
deportment, etc. The possibilities for antagonism and conflict
were endless. Trouble could also arise between parishioners over
choir robes, a too-high curb by the too-expensive parking lot, and
the inevitable question: "Will giving too much support for
'others overseas' mean less service for ME?"

One such instance stands out as clearly as if it had just been
concluded last Tuesday. There was a charismatic explosion that
blew 125 members right out of the church across town into a blue
steel Butler building that had formerly been a warehouse. It went
something like this. First, a rather ordinary, standard, run-of-
the-mill minister had been swept up in an enthusiastic in-dwelling
of the Holy Spirit. He then ardently desired that his church
council should also be able to speak in tongues, having the gifts of
interpretation of tongues as well as dramatic capacities for instant
healing by the same Spirit. Before you could say "Amen," the
congregation divided into pro and con. (You recall my saying

earlier that I had learned no group is so small they should not divide at least into two parts.)

Now I am certainly not against blessings; but I do become concerned when they cause inordinate trouble and the Fire of the Holy Spirit turns into a prairie fire amidst the fellowship. Some seized with glee upon the text for last Sunday, which reads (according to Luke 12:52) thus:

> From now on five in one household will be divided,
> three against two and two against three:
>> father against son
> mother against daughter
>> and daughter against mother,
> mother-in-law against her
>> daughter-in-law
> and daughter-in-law against
>> mother-in-law.

As I entered a Bible class just in time to hear Satan whispering to a young man, "Hey, here's a perfect justification for having that big fuss with your old man you've been waiting for," I knew we were in trouble. The second clue to the conundrum of cleavage was in the pastor's office in the newly-built church. The heating and air conditioning controls were in his room and evidently under his control. Now he was to adjust the spiritual temperature of the members as well as their temporal temperature. A spiritual Sherlock Holmes I was not, but some things seemed obvious.

Being a burden bearer is especially a heavy job for a person with a congenitally weak back. Ten years before, bed rest had provided relief for my low back, disc problem, but now it began to return. Just because I had written and lectured about psychosomatic connections between religion and health does not mean I had it all together. I could diagnose the difficulty of others with the "Holier-than-thou" syndrome; but I seemed oblivious of my own "Humbler-than-thou" problem, which really means one is so innocent that nothing bad could possibly happen. Actually these are two sides of the same coin. Be that as it may, let me tell you what happened to me. As the six-months stint of restoring the congregation's health progressed well, my back got worse. The last few Sundays I would shoehorn myself into the car and start the engine by turning the ignition key, which did not affect my back in any way. By the time I got to the church it took me about five minutes of leaning on the hood of the car before I could straighten up to an at least respectable slouch. I would smilingly greet the folks as I carried my regalia into the church office, but wisely did not sit down, since I would not be able to get up again if I did. The parishioners respected my religiosity since they saw me almost exclusively standing or kneeling, but surely not sitting. To make a long story short, I had slipped disc surgery a few days after the going-away potluck. The Epistle of last Sunday rounds out the story:

> My child, do not regard lightly
>   the discipline of the Lord,
> or lose heart when you are
>   punished by him;
> for the Lord disciplines those
>   whom he loves,
> and chastises every child
>   whom he accepts.

And I still remembered from my Speech Clinic days that I had indeed been accepted. Who was it who said, "Physician, heal thyself"?

A more successful case of mind over matter was the time I was scheduled to preach on the very day I came down with the stomach flu. Undaunted by my motto, learned from circus high wire acts, "The show must go on," I threw up only twice on my way to the church, stopping the car in time not to get digestive material all over the door. There I was fully robed in white surplice and gleaming red and gold stole waiting for the prelude to end so I could make my grand entry into the chancel. Fortunately the window opened easily so I could lean out the window far enough not to get anything on my nice outfit. Licking my lips one more time to make sure I was presentable, I began the service with no spasm of either the speech mechanism or the stomach. In a leisurely way, I greeted everyone at the door, got into the car carefully and headed down the road. When I was well out of sight of the remaining chatters, I stopped once more, headed for the ditch, leaned over, and felt much better after that. I may have missed a speaking engagement sometime in my life due to illness, but I am hardpressed to remember it. If you should hear about it, please let me know since I am eager to follow Saint Paul's admonition to "think not more highly of yourself than you ought to think." That tricky comparative adjective again.

Another case of the church conflict comes to mind, in which, by the testimony of all concerned, I had been therapeutically helpful. Surgery was limited to Sundays because I was teaching full-time back at the University and refused to make more than one trip a week. The minister had been eased out with acrimonious accusations and counter-thrusts. I reminded me of Papa. In some church windows there should be a picture of two persons in dueling outfits, mask on face and rapier in hand. During an adult Sunday School class, I tossed out this idea: "As I was driving into town, I had a strange vision. I saw that a tornado had swept through only this one spot and blown this church away, bricks, altar, pews and all, and scattered the debris over a dozen corn fields." Then I posed my question. "What do

you believe the rest of the townsfolk would think about this?"
Some allowed as how the Methodists would let them use their
church Sunday afternoons. There would be much support and
help and concern from all sides. I took a different turn. "Maybe
they would say, 'Now with that church gone, there isn't as much
fighting in town as there used to be.'" First, their jaws dropped
and they were in a state of shock. Then gradually, some smiled
and others laughed. The ice was broken. The cat was out of the
bag. We might just as well deal with it. Naturally, I did not pull
this until I had been there a few weeks and established a good
relationship and had given them time to tell me how grateful they
were to Dr. Belgum, His Honor, the Rev. Professor, so much
appreciated.

I will not bore you with further examples of continuing
education, but should turn now to how I dealt with the question of
retirement at age 65.

CHAPTER XVIII

BACK TO ANOTHER BETHANY

My prospects turned out to be the best a person in my station in life could ever hope for. A year to the day from the time I began my retirement on New Year's Day, 1988, I commenced a new work on January 1, 1989. I preached in the pulpit of Bethany Lutheran Church in West Branch, a short ten miles east of Iowa City. It is just across the Johnson County line, a kind of symbolic new frontier to cross. Several reasons make this an ideal vocation for me in my retirement and indicate why these last reflections are my most positive ones.

1. *Size Within my Scope.* One hundred eighty confirmed members are so much more manageable than eighty thousand souls, including that guy in the Oxford bar and the garage gang. Within a few short years I should be able to learn many of the names of these dear people. They are so congenial and forgiving that I am truly at peace among them. Every now and then I am congratulated by a friend for not winning the county election when an unusually messy conflict with a developer is reported in the *Iowa City Press-Citizen.*

2. *Mentally Manageable.* It is true that at Bethany I am required to turn in a term paper a week, in fact deliver it orally each Sunday at 10:00 a.m., more or less in the form of a sermon. These are generally limited to somewhere between fifteen and twenty minutes, far less than my learned journal articles with their required three footnotes per page. Each one is supposed to be a balance of theory and practice, which makes them really fun and challenging to prepare. They like them to be "useful," a refreshing change from some of my friends in academe.

3. *Rural and Real.* Maybe one of the attractions about working
for the county is that so much of it is outdoors. I've always
appreciated the First Article of the Creed where it tells about "...
the Almighty, maker of heaven and earth, and of all things visible
and invisible." In a small town surrounded by farms, hills,
valleys, creeks, trees, wildflowers, and wildlife of all kinds,
nature seems so immediate and present to one's senses. After
working amidst the bureaucracy and technology of University
Hospital or sitting through the gyrations of a faculty or staff
meeting, I always found it refreshing to go out to our acreage and
check on the Black Angus, the potatoes and onions, and hear the
songs of two or three kinds of birds. It cleansed the mind as well
as the soul. That is what West Branch and environs can do for
me. It keeps me in touch with reality: Life and death, the
wonders of nature, the dynamic, changing, yet ever dependable
seasons.

4. *Sociability and Socialism.* It was Danish immigrants who
settled in southwest Cedar County and founded Bethany Church.
They came from one of the several Scandinavian countries
famous for successful and peaceful application of democratic
socialism. Perhaps this is why they would not have been turned
off if they had even guessed that their most recent pastor had been
Iowa's only Socialist mayor. To this day, the trademark of
Bethany is sociability, coffee and visiting after the Sunday
service, potlucks aplenty. Yes, social, sociability, socialism,
confraternity, call it what you will, it's at Bethany. Oh, they
don't go around calling themselves socialists in the political sense.
As in most American communities there are only two parties to
choose from: Democratic and Republican; but just below the
surface you'd find they are really social at heart.

5. *Sanity and Sanctity.* Like I pronounce from the pulpit
liturgically after every sermon: "The peace that passeth

understanding" is precious. It is ironic that I find sanity and sanctity in a Bethany founded by Danes in the last decade of the last century just like I did in another Bethany when I was doing my graduate study at Boston University. It was also founded by Danes in the last decade of the nineteenth century. That one was located in the slums of the Roxbury section of Boston. Maybe a person can find sanity and sanctity anywhere: In the city and in the country, on the town council and on the board of supervisors, in the university and in the church.

You may wonder why I find parish ministry so rewarding when countless people look at it as rather peripheral and many practitioners suffer from burnout. For me it goes back to my fascination with the connection between theory and practice, between faith and what gives meaning to life and actual behavior and life-style. High religion deals with the realities of life from the cradle to the grave and everything in between: self-image, motivation, relationships, ethics (both social and medical), family life, vocation with the attendant stewardship of one's capacities and opportunities. In short, there is hardly any area of life which is not influenced or shaped by one's religious orientation. Preaching in such a context is challenging to say the least.

Pastoral care of persons in stress situations of illness, broken relationships, dying and/or grief, success and failure is a rewarding opportunity to share in a significant way with people. Character and personality development of children and adolescents through religious education and group work is very important, especially conspicuous since both parties claim "values" as important in their political campaigns in this election year.

The more I studied the life cycle, especially as Erik Erikson laid it out, the more I saw religious perspective at each stage of life. What complicates the enterprise is that religion can be negative or positive, enhancing one's sense of worth and self-esteem or oppressing one with unresolved guilt and self-hatred.

Of course, there is a freshness to my ministry because I had not been in it fully for all those years when I was a professor. If I had been doing parish work for the last thirty-five years, it would no doubt be a heavier load that I would be eager to lay down. That is why I said in the first sentence of this chapter, "My prospects turned out to be the best a person in my station in life could ever hope for."

Ministry is a variable and flexible profession. It deals with joyous childbirth and bubbling childhood and the slowing down of old age with possible infirmity, yet rich with maturity and experiences. So much cannot be shared because it has happened under a commitment of confidentiality; but let me assure you this vocation is full of pathos and raucous humor, celebration and tragedy. It can be very formal yet intimate in sharing of feelings, moods, worries, and hopes.

Humor is constantly interspersed among serious business in the ministry, especially if you are open to it and don't take yourself too seriously. At a recent wedding, the couple wanted to make the four-year-old daughter of the bride feel included. As the man and woman had exchanged their rings, I was to call upon the little girl to come forward and receive a necklace. "Come here, we have something for you too." Immediately, from the fourth row came a voice from a boy cousin the same age, "I want something too." Fair is fair. At a funeral I misspoke the name of the widow until I finally got back on track. Afterwards I mentioned my mistake to ladies who were making the lunch for the reception following committal at the grave. "Yes," one replied, "Several times." Then I sought out the widow, who was by now sitting near a vacant chair. I approached with my coffee cup in hand and sat down. "Hazel," I began, "I made a mistake and called you Mabel. Did you notice that?" She smiled forgivingly and said, "No, I didn't; but several people pointed it out to me."

The role is fraught with the pitfalls of administration and group leadership. I assured the members of this latter Bethany that I might easily offend two people a month; so if I were around long enough I would get around to everyone. There is no way of being too skilled at oratory or too profound in scholarship providing the preacher really makes connection with the parishioners where they are really living their lives.

I meet my people in the front of the Post Office and in their homes, in the hospital and in nursing homes. I see the young people at some sports events or town affairs. The work is always different from day to day, never a dull moment; yet the basics need tending each week. Sometimes I can be as cool as a cucumber under pressure; and then again I can get a catch in my throat as I pray for the blessing of God upon a family leaving us for another city, vocation and social engagement. Funerals have always been very meaningful, a strategic time when support of both social and eternal dimensions is needed. And "underneath are the Everlasting Arms supporting us all the day long."

Counseling in cases of disturbed marriage and divorce can be very frustrating since often the decision and answer have been formed in the mind of one or both before the questions have even been properly framed. Sometimes one can become cynical. One can get the feeling that the only reason for coming for so-called "marriage counseling" is to be able to tell Mama, "I tried everything; I even went to see the minister." Yet one must refrain from judgmentalism and the danger of rejecting another human being out of hand, while at the same time remaining objective and somewhat diagnostic in one's approach to the problems unfolding.

For me, the two Bethanys are like two sets of quotation marks bracketing my career. I'm glad I passed this way.

POSTSCRIPT

In writing one's autobiography, timing is a tricky matter. One must wait long enough until the case history is almost finished; but if one waits too long it is too late. I have no way of knowing whether publishing this on the verge of my 70th birthday is much too early. What if I live to be 95? Then this report will be covering only about three-fourths of my life's journey, hardly a complete case record. So, take it for what it is worth, just my account of what my life has meant to me thus far.

Like Abraham, I did not know where I was destined to end up when God called, "Go from your country and your kindred and your father's house to the land that I will show you." Nor did I really know for sure what would happen when I followed the ancient admonition, "Therefore a man leaves his father and his mother and cleaves to his wife, and they become one flesh." I now believe that <u>faith</u> means "not having to know." Thus faith reduced my anxiety a lot. I was constantly confronted by new openings not of my own making. You recall that several times I said I saw the handwriting on the wall, and I had a choice to heed it or not.

Saint Paul accepted the end of his life with equanimity even though he was writing from prison and had no idea how long he had yet to live. He wrote, "whether we live or whether we die, we are the Lord's." Whenever I have felt I was the Lord's, that is when I felt best about my life and work. Paul wrote to a young pastor this testimony, which I also make my own:

> I am now ready to be offered, and the time of my departure is at hand. I have fought a good fight, I have finished my course, I have kept the faith: henceforth there is laid up for me a crown of righteousness, which the Lord, the righteous Judge, shall give me at that day: and not to me only, but unto all them also that love his appearing. *(II Timothy 4:6-8)*

Dear Reader: I want to thank you for accompanying me on this long journey. Maybe it has been as useful for you as for me. The younger generation has a word for it: "Get it all together." As I said before, I find this passage from Psalm 90 helpful and meaningful: "So teach us to number our days, that we may apply our hearts unto wisdom." Although we have so often heard this admonition read during a funeral service, we need not wait for a crisis to reflect on the significance of the past, present and future of our lives. Whenever we thus meditate, we gain some more wisdom, understanding, and insight. In the eternal scheme of things, anyone can say, as I've said, "Excuse me, I'm just passing by."

POST POSTSCRIPT

Hey! I'm back. Yes, it was about FIVE years ago when I thought I had finished my story; but some interesting things have happened since my second retirement--this time from Bethany Church in West Branch, after about six years of ministry in what had begun supposedly as an "interim." Also, after a gradual decline in health and energy, my brother, Joe, died about a year ago in Montana where he and Esther had lived in a very pleasant retirement. At the funeral, Sister Dorothy and I were reflective about how our family had now been reduced to just the two of us.

THREE PROJECTS

Since I last talked to you, I decided to make a video series under the title: DEALING WITH THE DARK SIDE OF LIFE. It was aired over our local public access television channel. What really pleased me was the fact that the College of Nursing now lists it as available for continuing education units for nurses.

I. SHAME:

Deviance
Stigma
How to Deal With
  Shame & Stigma

II. GUILT:

Many Kinds
Hypocracy
A Functional
  Confessional

III. SUFFERING:

Why Me?
How Is It
  Experienced?
What Does It Mean?

IV. SICKNESS:

Medical Ethics
Your Turn To
  Decide
Dying & Grieving

This was the first time I had tried to do anything with TV; and I found out it is a whole new world out there. How to keep the program from simply being a talking head lecture? It was not easy. I prepared some placards, or replaced one picture on a card with another illustration. Then there were interviews with therapists as well as clients. Nevertheless, it did not have the fast pace of a Ford pickup ad where each image is on screen anywhere from one to two-and-a-half seconds as the announcer crisply says "corners well," "handles any weather," and "solid comfort."

I gave TV a second look, as we so often do once we get involved with something we had only criticized at a distance. It is really not necessary to have five minutes of a Ford pickup coming around twelve different corners to get across the message, "corners well." Lecturers and some preachers take a long, long time getting to the point:

> Last week, when I began to wonder how I should approach our topic today, actually a part of a larger series that will be on-going throughout the week, it occurred to me that, at this point in time, there are so many factors that could impinge upon our discussion, depending, of course, upon the philosophical, or even ethnological perspectives that each of us bring to this topic, which, as many before me have said, makes this issue so perplexing.

Would I dare to go back and listen to the tapes of my radio lectures after having had this conversion experience?

What did happen was that my appetite for television as a medium for education was whetted. Both Tom Nothnagle, my camera man, and I became aware of what we would have to do to make the end product more professional and effective. How could we compete with the University Video Center, which would lend technical services, but at the cost of $1,000 a minute. It was then that I noticed the number of staff listed after some documentary program, several cameras from different angles, sound crews with color coordinators, script writers, directors, editors, etc., etc. The end product is then really smooth.

I learned that TV script writing has to follow a double track: one for the audio script and another for the visuals, plus a precise time allocation in between. I had a bunch of sheets duplicated as follows:

<u>Script Sequence</u>	for	Program: _______ Page #: _______
<u>VISUALS</u> (any image, symbol, picture, photo or action video shots)	<u>TIME</u> (in minutes & seconds)	<u>AUDIO</u> (any spoken monologue dialogue, special sound effects, music, etc.)

If there turned out to be a very long stretch of talk without some visual support, I'd hear from my editor. This format provided good discipline and balance. I really had to think about what I was doing and why. Is this part necessary, etc.?

The theme of this next series is CULTURAL DIVERSITY: Fabrics of Society. It is designed for high school students and covers eight different culture groups: Czech, Jewish, Islam, African Americans, Native Americans, Asians, Norwegians, Old Order Amish, and Hispanics. Among the six endorsements on the back cover of the book, the Executive Director of the Iowa Humanities Board said that it would be "sure to stimulate not only lively discussion in adult and family-based study/discussion groups but also deeper pursuit of the cultural meanings of our rich and varied ethnic landscape." I suggested this cover to a publisher:

A ten-minute video accompanies each chapter of the text and should assist the teacher in initiating discussion about each group in turn.

I was fortunate to obtain the skilled services of Bruce Drummond of the instructional Media Production Laboratory at the College of Education in the University of Iowa. His critique, editorial sensitivity and advice were very valuable. The end product was a great leap forward from "The Dark Side of Life." Even then, Tom and I kept on learning out in the field. When we arrived at a Jewish home where we would learn about how a kosher kitchen is run, the hostess graciously asked if we would like coffee. "Yes, thank you." Later we heard the coffee percolator being carefully picked up on our sensitive microphone. Oh, well, we said it was a kitchen. Instead, we had it re-taped in the kitchen of the synagogue.

Something far more significant than technique arose in this enterprise. As I tried hard to listen to and sensitively understand the unique story of each one of these diverse cultures, the broader my vision and the deeper my sensitivity became. Remember how I described the narrow parochialism of my childhood in the Norwegian Lutheran rural ghetto of central Minnesota? Now I was not only embracing Swedish Lutherans and a stray Methodist. Here, sixty years later, I was appreciating Muslims and riding to an Old Order Amish funeral in a buggy of the Church District Bishop; glad to be participating in a jubilant and spontaneous African American Church service; and actually feeling very welcome and comfortable as Kathie and I were guests at the Seder meal at the local synagogue.

Had I really become that loose around the edges or just been around state universities too long? I began a serious study of the dramatically new movement of trans-cultural ecumenism. The basic question is quite simple: "Is it possible to hold firmly and faithfully to one's own heritage without needing to denigrate and despise what is so totally "other?" I found myself not only being more empathetic toward groups quite different from my own; I began to appreciate where they were coming from and why they thought as they thought and did what they did.

What a new age we live in. A pope gently referred to Protestants as "separated brethren"--certainly a long jump from the days of the Spanish Inquisition. The folks in New England have given up burning witches (i.e., those who deviated from the norm); and we have considerably slowed down our genocide of Native Americans and talk less vociferously about our "manifest destiny." Another papal statement refers to a more sympathetic relation with "non-Christian religion."

Cardinal Ratzinger made the following presentation in Hong Kong:

> "... culture, is the historically developed common form of expression of the insights and values which characterize the life of a community ...."

He goes on to speak about the need to "... understand better the possible inter-communication of cultures ..." (ORIGINS, Volume 24, No. 41, March 30, 1995, p.680).

Note two items: first the "other" culture the Church wishes to address also has "insights" and values" and are hence not to be considered a completely worthless society; and second, there is to be "inter-communication," a dialogue instead of a one way monologue. On the following page he explains further:

> "For this reason, we should no longer speak of inculturation but of the meeting of cultures or interculturality, to coin a new phrase. For inculturation presumes that a faith stripped of culture whereby two subjects, formally unknown to each other, meet and fuse."

Here is mutual respect, dialogue and sharing--how different from the one-way traffic relations when Columbus and his followers dealt with natives in Central and South America. I am glad and encouraged by statements of openness, respect and mutuality. Those early soldiers and missionaries not only disapproved of the natives' religion, but were disgusted by their food, clothing and entire life style.

I come back to my question: "Is it possible to hold firmly and faithfully to one's own heritage without needing to denigrate, hate or despise what is totally "other?" Consider this analogy. Two people observe a tennis ball; one says it is fuzzy and the other says it is round. Three see another ball. One says it is black, another says it is heavy, and a third says it has three holes in it. Of course, it is all three because it is a bowling ball. A more careful and objective view may observe that various religions, cultures may view the Creator, what is sacred, what is required for the good life and social order from different perspectives, yet all dealing with the same reality (at least approximately so).

This does not mean that I glibly say anything that happens is OK, because that is just how that group is. I am still horrified by the worship of Moloch, which a dictionary defines as "a deity, mentioned in the Bible, whose worship marked by the burning of children offered as a propitiatory sacrifice by their parents." I hope we can agree that some things are a blessing and others definitely a curse. As society matures ethically, many things that were once accepted are now illegal: child abuse, slavery, to name only two. But I have talked about these two projects long enough.

If writing short stories in my retirement was good, then writing a novel should be that much better. So I did. It is entitled YONDER FORK and describes the life, tribulations and victories of a boy/man of Norwegian descent living about thirty miles Northwest of Minneapolis. He spends time in a mental hospital as a "disturbed and incorrigible youth," accepts "client status" in a Speech Clinic and generally makes good use of resources, so he grows and matures into a successful person. His good marriage to a gypsy refugee is very compatible. The story is very optimistic. If it is published, I hope you'll enjoy it.

Oh, yes, I must not forget to announce my second novel: BOY FROM NOWHERE. Since I had written about "Cultural Diversity," I thought I should write about a boy who had no ethnic identification whatsoever. His parents were lost at sea, and no trace of his national original was discovered in the stateroom. It was a most rewarding self-assignment. I leave it to your imagination what problems this causes him later in life

Sometimes I would wake up early with a start wondering what would happen to Daniel today. Then he'd tell me and I could continue writing.

Both Daniel in this story and Thor in the first novel had difficult problems to confront, but instead of resorting to violence, like in so many contemporary stories; they made good decisions and took constructive actions. They also made good use of resources. They are deliberately positive role models for any youth who will read them.

Meanwhile I write an essay or two on some subject no one else had gotten around to yet, which may or may not be published. But at least I have read them and benefited from them. Never too old to learn, even from yourself.

What has all this to do with my retirement, you may ask? I believe retirement provides new opportunities to pursue goals and projects not outlined in our job description, or the company's policy and procedure manual, as useful as these may be in their place. There is a freedom to experiment since in retirement you really don't have to prove anything. If cultural diversity never gets accepted by a commercial publisher, the project would still be very much worth it because of what I've learned and the interesting contacts/relationships I've had in these diverse settings. I've bought more books, spent more of my own money, and talked with more people on this project than I have concerning any course I ever taught in seminary or university.

I worry about the heroic protection against "ageism" whereby professors and other professionals do not have a mandatory retirement age. The old professor meets his student in mid-campus and asks "Was I coming from my office or from the library?" "You were coming from your office, Professor." "Oh, good, then I've had lunch." If senility creeps into the pulpit or behind the lecture podium, it is there for all to see and be embarrassed about. If you're slipping and writing a book which shows signs of "ageism," to put it politely, the publisher simply thanks you for sending them this piece, "but it does not fit into our current publishing program." And no one is the wiser. Anyone who cannot accept aging gracefully makes both self and others miserable and uncomfortable.

I hope what I learned in the Speech Clinic fifty years ago will still stand me in good stead. "Accept yourself." I had better accept myself since I turned 75 during the 1988 Christmas holidays.

Oh, one last item. You are wondering about the status of the family at this writing. The following photo was taken at a luau in Hawaii where we celebrated our 45th wedding anniversary.

At the left are Gretchen and Kurt with their two, Erik and Kate in front. Next are Grandpa and Grandma. Veronique is holding their little Chloe with Karl at her side. Finally Kit is holding Morgan and Forrest is in charge of Mariah. A great family and a lot of fun.